Integrated
Robotics

Ian Chow-Miller

Cavendish
Square

New York

Published in 2017 by Cavendish Square Publishing, LLC
243 5th Avenue, Suite 136, New York, NY 10016

Website: cavendishsq.com

This publication represents the opinions and views of the author based on his or her personal experience, knowledge, and research. The information in this book serves as a general guide only. The author and publisher have used their best efforts in preparing this book and disclaim liability rising directly or indirectly from the use and application of this book.

CPSIA Compliance Information: Batch #CW17CSQ

All websites were available and accurate when this book was sent to press.

Names: Chow-Miller, Ian.
Title: Integrated robotics / Ian Chow-Miller.
Description: New York : Cavendish Square Publishing, [2017] | Series:
Robotics | Includes bibliographical references and index.
Identifiers: LCCN 2016021848 (print) | LCCN 2016029636 (ebook) |
ISBN 9781502619365 (library bound) | ISBN 9781502619372 (E-book)
Subjects: LCSH: Robots--Design and construction--Juvenile literature. |
Robots--Programming--Juvenile literature. | Robotics--Juvenile literature.
Classification: LCC TJ211.2 .C5343 2017 (print) | LCC TJ211.2 (ebook) |
DDC 629.8/92--dc23

LC record available at https://lccn.loc.gov/2016021848

Editorial Director: David McNamara
Editor: Fletcher Doyle
Copy Editor: Nathan Heidelberger
Assistant Art Director: Amy Greenan
Designer: Alan Sliwinski
Production Coordinator: Karol Szymczuk
Photo Research: J8 Media

The photographs in this book are used by permission and through the courtesy of: Cover Yougen/iStock.com; p. 4 Ethan Miller/Getty Images Entertainment/Getty Images; p. 8 Used with permission from Parallax Inc. Copyright © 2016 Parallax Inc. All rights reserved; p. 10 Lego Mindstorms RCX, photographed by Mairi/File:LegoMindstormsRCX.jpg/Wikimedia Commons; p. 13, 22, 69 Courtesy Vex Robotics; p. 15 Bloomberg/Getty Images; p. 16 MARK RALSTON/Getty Images; pp. 18, 31, 34, 37, 44, 50-51, 54, 59, 60, 77, 83, 86: Ian Chow-Miller; p. 21 hew J. Lee/The Boston Globe/Getty Images; p. 28 isafx/iStock/Thinkstock; p. 32 Julija Sapic/Shutterstock.com; p. 33 JakeUM/File:Underwater Linear Actuator.png/Wikimedia Commons; p. 39 Jeopardy Productions via Getty Images; p. 42 Denys Po/Shutterstock.com; p. 40 Maxisport/Shutterstock.com; p. 57 flixelhouse/Shutterstock.com; p. 62 rjp/flickr.com; p. 66 Autoine Taveneaux/File:Cage de Faraday.jpg/Wikimedia Commons; p. 70 EVARISTO SA/Getty Images; p. 79 erfectlab/Shutterstock.com; p. 81 NASA; p. 88 Chris Bartle/File:Roomba time-lapse.jpg/Wikimedia Commons; p. 90 Westend61/Getty Images.

Printed in the United States of America

Contents

BB-8, a fictional robot, captivated millions of young moviegoers the way R2-D2 did a generation earlier.

1 What Is a Robot?

Think for a second and picture the first thing that comes to mind when you hear the word **robot**. Is it BB-8? Or, if you're older like me, perhaps it's C-3PO or R2-D2? Or does a vacuum roaming around the floor of your living room picking up dust with nobody holding the handle fit the bill? Maybe it's an unmanned **drone** dropping bombs on the enemy, or it could be an industrial robot making cars in a factory. While we all might have different images of a robot, I'm willing to bet that most people, and especially most people reading this book, have some solid concept of what a robot is.

If we all have an idea of what a robot is, why do we all have such different ideas? In researching this book, I've looked up over a dozen different definitions of robots, and they all differ in some respects. This is because the word "robot" is not one that has developed over hundreds of years. It doesn't have an etymology that can be traced to an ancient Latin root that has sprouted tons of words familiar to readers of the English language today. Instead, "robot" was coined by a Czech playwright named Karel Čapek. He wrote a play in 1921 called

R.U.R. (subtitled *Rossum's Universal Robots*). The "robots" in his play were artificially manufactured humans who were produced to do work. The word "robot" most likely comes from the Czech word *robota*, which translates as "forced servitude."

The robots of classic science fiction started the trend toward the **anthropomorphic robot** and probably not only spawned C-3PO but also gave the idea to many a young boy or girl to dress up for Halloween in a cardboard box wrapped in aluminum foil with buttons glued on. Yours truly was one of them.

But we know that these walking humanoids are not the only type of robots out there. Outside of the movies, there are actually very few of them compared to other types of robots, though they are becoming more prevalent. So how do we define "robot" and what fits into our definition? The definition I like to use, and one that seems to cover most of the robots we will examine in this book is: a programmable mechanical device (usually electronic) that carries out a series of automated tasks.

This definition allows us to include all the robots discussed in this book, including drones, industrial robots, those little roaming vacuums, and many others. But it also allows us to include a dishwasher. Is a dishwasher a robot? Programmable? Check. Mechanical device? Check. Carries out a series of automated tasks? Check. So if your dishwasher is a robot, what about your coffee machine? Hmmm … the waters can get muddied.

Working Definition

A word that originates in a play, is picked up by Hollywood, and can be applied to almost any modern machine quickly loses its power to specifically define something. For this book, instead of trying to come up with a working definition of robot, I am going to narrow the scope to **educational robots**. These are the focus of this book, and since they are an area in which I have familiarity and expertise, I can provide us with a working definition that will lay the foundation for our further exploration.

An educational robot is one that is designed to be programmable by a student. It is small and inexpensive enough to meet the logistical and economic requirements of school teams and classes. It is nonspecific in its design, meaning it is not meant to mimic or emulate only one or two types of machines, but it can be built into hundreds if not thousands of different types of machines, with infinite variations.

Most educational robots are plug and play. Cables will easily connect motors and sensors with the brain. They won't require soldering or building a circuit board or other specialized engineering skills. While these are important and fun to learn, they shouldn't be a requirement for those who wish to learn how to build and program robots. There is a small subsection of educational robots in which the kit that students first build from does require putting together pieces under the hood, so to speak. One of these is the BoeBot (www.parallax.com), and while they are becoming popular, they don't come close to commanding anywhere near the market share that other educational robotics systems do.

If there's one company that has been at the forefront of bringing robots to the classroom and to an entire generation of students, it's LEGO Education, with VEX Robotics running a close second. LEGO Education got the ball moving with its

The BoeBot offers an alternative to most robots aimed at the educational market. An open chassis allows you to wire all the jumper cables, attach the processor, and connect LEDs, resistors, and transistors.

first robot, the LEGO Mindstorms RCX (which stood for Remote Control Explorer) released in 1998.

The RCX had studs on the top and stud holes on the bottom with only a few pin holes on the side, which meant that a lot of the building was done with traditional LEGO pieces (meaning plates and bricks) as opposed to the LEGO Technic pieces (such as **beams, axles,** and connector pins) that their newer robots come with almost exclusively. The differences between the RCX and newer models didn't stop at building pieces.

The brain of the robot, referred to as the RCX Brick, could hold a maximum of five programs (a few of which were default programs that had to be overwritten if you wanted to use that space). It had three motor **ports** and three sensor ports. And frustratingly, programs were downloaded using an infrared tower that was connected to your computer via USB. Programs would take a while to download, and if you had to update the firmware, that could take several agonizingly long minutes or more. We used to have to put a shoebox over the IR Tower and robot to shield it from outside light. Sometimes the process would reach seventy or eighty percent completion only to fail and need to be restarted.

Still, the RCX was a great robot for learning with and definitely fit my definition of an "educational robot." It could be programmed with software provided by LEGO Education named Robotics Invention System and later it was programmable with Robolab, a software program developed by Tufts University CEEO (Center for Engineering Education Outreach) and based on the venerable LabVIEW software from National Instruments. My first year teaching robotics and my first year coaching FIRST LEGO League was with the RCX. Even though it was a first model, the RCX could do a lot. My neophyte programmers and builders managed to knock the space dust off a solar panel, retrieve ice cores, launch a projectile, and save the Mars Rover in our first competitive year using the RCX.

In 2006, LEGO Education released the NXT (NeXT robot, get it?), which was a significant upgrade from the RCX. The NXT was clearly designed to be a part of the Technic building system, it came with its own eponymous software, there were three motor and four sensor ports, and it connected to the computer via a USB cable for very quick downloading of programs. The NXT also had available, for the first time, onboard programming capabilities (meaning no computer needed).

LEGO Education made the move with the NXT to make its hardware and software open-source. This decision, which was gutsy at the time, allowed developers to write their own languages to run on the NXT, and allowed other companies to create third-party sensors for the NXT. Ultimately this paid off by expanding the NXT's popularity and usability. LEGO Education continued its open-source ways with the 2013 release of its current robotic platform, the EV3.

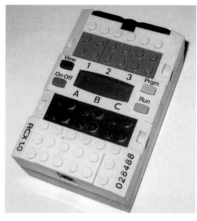

The RCX was the first programmable brick from LEGO Education.

This third evolution (EVolution3) of LEGO Education robots includes more great improvements. It has four sensor and four motor ports, two different kinds of motors, more building pieces in the kit, more colors among the pieces (NXT was mainly dull gray), vastly improved Bluetooth capability, new software (again eponymously named), expanded memory, and a host of other features. While somewhat mitigated by a difficult-to-read screen, the EV3 rocks the robotic house in most ways.

I am not here to compare one system to another. There are plenty of articles on the Internet that do so, and what you'll find is that, as with most things, people tend to favor what they are used to. I have used LEGO Education robots more than VEX because they have been supplied to me by the schools where I work. I certainly am not buying them all myself. So my preferences are swayed. While LEGO Education has decades of experience with its parent company, LEGO, that helps it make quality products in a timely fashion, there are quite a few other robotics products to look at. Let's start with VEX.

VEX has been around for about a decade as of 2016. Originally, the line of products started as part of the FIRST suite of competitions (called FIRST VEX Challenge) but eventually branched out on its own into competition and classroom products. This line of products is referred to as VEX EDR (Educational Robots), and is a few steps above the NXT/EV3 in complexity. The VEX building system is made out of all-metal structural parts with a lot of high-strength plastic **gears**, strong plastic wheels, and other strong parts. It's meant to be built using nuts, bolts, washers, spacers, stand-offs, and other parts that mimic machinery. It is not a simple snap-and-click system like LEGO Technic.

Another major way in which it differs is in the brain itself, the VEX Cortex. The Cortex has no screen or buttons, other than an on/off switch. It also has separate ports for analog and digital sensors as well as motors; these ports require careful placing of easily bendable pins at the end of wires into tiny holes. These connections are not simple "phone jack" styles but require care and precision. This is not a bad thing and is very realistic, but it is the reason why the VEX Cortex is mainly aimed at upper grades. (I use it with my eighth graders but would not drop it down to my sixth-grade class, for example.) The other major difference with the VEX Cortex is the programming environment.

The VEX EDR used to be programmed mainly using RobotC, a **text-based** computer language based on the C family of programming languages. It is not a particularly difficult language for an aspiring roboticist, but as it involves text, any **syntax** mistake will cause your program not to work.

This can be frustrating for the novice and for the teacher who may have a class of thirty or more students, not all of whom wish to become expert programmers. RobotC has two workarounds they've developed. The first was a "Natural Language" version that was developed to be used by Project Lead the Way (PLTW) classes. PLTW is a nationwide organization that has developed a popular suite of STEM courses, some of which include a unit on Automation and Robotics. Along with teaching robotics classes, I am also a PLTW-licensed teacher. The "Natural Language" version of RobotC simplifies some of the syntax commands so there are not so many errors and the frustration level is lessened for everyone. I have found it very helpful to use with my PLTW classes. But RobotC went even further in making its software user friendly, creating a graphical version of their software which avoided the syntax errors of its text-based counterpart.

A few years ago, VEX released its new kit, VEX IQ. Clearly aimed at middle school and even upper elementary classes, this system has gained in popularity recently. Containing plastic pieces and some connectors similar to LEGO Technic, it would be unfair to both companies to call them a copy. The larger IQ pieces are designed to flex, which allows you to connect them in some interesting ways you wouldn't be able to do with LEGO. While the system started out in mainly grey and maroon pieces, VEX quickly responded to customer desires with lots of color.

The features of VEX IQ are more than surface appearance, though. The brain of the system, called the VEX IQ Robot Brain, has twelve ports, which are not specifically designed for sensors or motors, accepting either in any open port. This makes building easy, as you don't have to worry about brain orientation in making room for wires to fit. The sensors the IQ comes with are very similar to the EV3's, with the exception of a Touch LED. These little guys can be programmed to light up in different colors when touched but also act as buttons that can be used to help convey messages to the robot. Just touch one with your finger and the Touch LED may glow green, and you can send your robot on its way. When VEX IQ was first released, the company also touted the ability to program with a free program called Modkit, which is yet another **graphical programming environment**.

There are a large number of companies or individuals looking to design a new robotics system and bring it on the market. These will fit in with the already crowded field. This book could be an exhaustive bore if I were to cover all of them; instead, to conclude this chapter, I will just feature a few more. I have already mentioned the BoeBot, and the next one that

Improvments such as the inclusion of twelve ports were made in the new VEX IQ (left), an update of the original VEX EDR robotics system (right).

comes to mind is Edison (www.meetedison.com). Edison is designed to be a cheaper alternative to other robotics kits. It does this well by cutting some smart corners. It contains no building pieces. Instead, it has a number of studs and stud holes on it to make it LEGO compatible. We all have some LEGO pieces laying around somewhere, right? Edison also has free software to program it with. All the sensors are built onto the bot—nothing to attach. And one very smart move they made is the use of a 2.5-millimeter audio wire for downloading programs. No USB, no expensive Bluetooth or Wi-Fi capability. This enables you to program with your iPad as well. Of course the robots are limited in that you can't position sensors or build a massive robot.

Two building systems that were designed to take advantage of the open-source nature of LEGO Education robots are Tetrix and Matrix. Despite similar-sounding names, different companies produce them. Both are designed to use an EV3 or NXT as the **controller**, but as the building system uses stronger metal components, you are expected to add motor controllers and use high-strength motors. Because of the advanced capability of the build system, it is more common to find someone programming these robots with RobotC or LabVIEW rather than EV3 or NXT software. The FIRST Tech Challenge allows both of these systems, though the companies moved on from an NXT controller to using Android Phones and an MIT app development environment in 2015.

Finally, at the other end of the spectrum are robots like the BeeBot, which is designed for very young students (I use it with my six-year-old), and LEGO WeDo, which is really

To meet consumer demand, most modern educational robot platforms can be programmed with devices like tablets and phones.

great for early elementary grades. BeeBot only has onboard programming and no building system other than three different color shells, but WeDo can take advantage of all the LEGO pieces out there and has its own software system.

When choosing a robotics system, you have to consider what your needs and goals are as well as what your budget is. All of the above options have their advantages and drawbacks. The important thing is that you get the product that suits you the best. If it's a vacuum cleaner roaming the floor of your house, freeing your parents from housework; a smarter search-and-rescue bot; or a robot to play cards with, you can build and program a prototype with VEX, LEGO, Tetrix, etc. Each of these will help you learn sound engineering skills, solid programming techniques, and allow your imagination to take you anywhere it wants to go. When you're done, you will have designed a programmable electromechanical device that carries out a series of automated tasks.

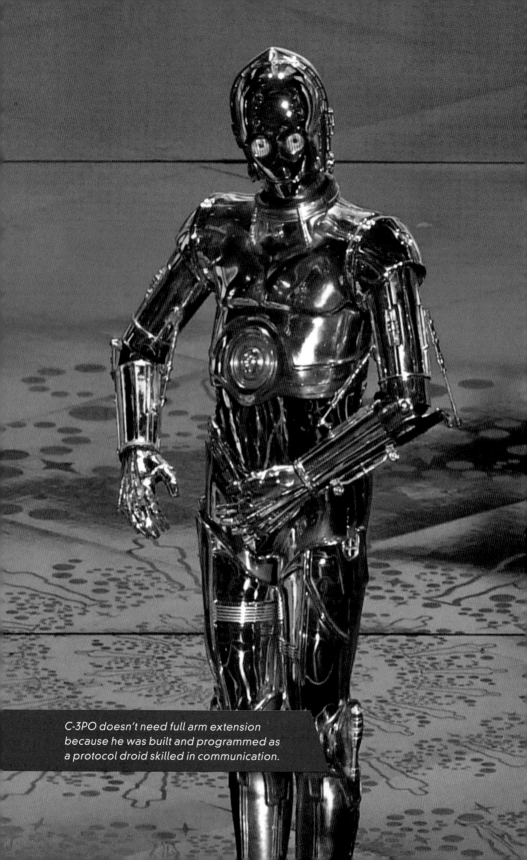

C-3PO doesn't need full arm extension because he was built and programmed as a protocol droid skilled in communication.

2 What's in a Robot

C-3PO, the droid from Star Wars, can barely move his arms. If you're a mega-fan of the Star Wars franchise (like I am), you probably know this already. A metal rod connects the inside of his "bicep" to the side of his "forearm." This severely limits his mobility. But once we consider that he is designed as a "protocol droid" who is fluent "in over six million forms of communication," we begin to see that full mobility in his arms is superfluous to his main function.

He was designed for a specific role and he fulfills that role really well. When we look at the **Roomba**, one of the more popular "robotic vacuums," we observe that it roams around the floor and sucks up dirt but doesn't have the ability to speak to us. Robots are built and programmed for specific reasons. Adding extra parts or functionality just because you can won't help, and may even hinder, the performance of your robot. They might drain battery power, get in the way, add weight, and require more complex programming, which can lead to more ways the robot can make mistakes.

When we look at competition-winning robots built by students, we notice that they maximize the use of motors and sensors and make the most of the allowable size as denoted by the competition rules. I have rarely seen an award-winning robot that is sparse or doesn't use most of the allowable parts; I have also not seen winning robots that contain extra or superfluous parts. They are built with exactly the pieces they need in order to score as many points as possible in the time allotted. Take a look at this robot from FIRST LEGO League's 2013 Nature's Fury challenge:

This LEGO robot looks very complex, but every part is used for a specific task; it maximizes efficiency as it goes about the board racking up points.

If we take a close look at this robot (*above*) we see there is a lot going on. Even from this one point of view, I can identify several interesting features. The first thing I notice is the orientation of the brain. A lot of teams and students tend to orient the brain so the motor ports and sensor ports are facing the front and back of the robot. Intuitively it feels right, but this is not always the best way to build. As a matter of fact, when you build like this you tend to artificially create a "front" and "back" of your robot, which can limit your ability to imagine ways it can perform. Your car is only built with a front because a physical driver needs to be able to see where he or she is going. All other considerations came after that.

In the image on page 18, you can also see four of the motor ports are being used. Two of those will be drive motors for the left and right side of the robot. The medium motor we can see on the left-hand side of the brain is operating a series of connected gears (including **spur gears** and **bevel gears**) that in turn are pumping the **piston** that is filling the air canister for the **pneumatics** while also connecting to the gear on the bottom right via the use of two **universal joints**. A fourth unseen motor is operating another mechanism elsewhere on the robot. (I know a fourth motor is being used because wires are connected to all four motor ports.) At least two of the sensor ports are being used, while the drive wheels at the back will smoothly turn the robot as it is resting on a castor wheel up front, most likely with one on the other side.

Systems

This is a complex robot, which is not the same as saying it is complicated. It has many features, but each is designed for a specific purpose and all parts work together in a cohesive whole. Trying to build a complex robot like this from scratch is difficult if we don't know what's what and aren't familiar with the different components and how they work together. In the rest of this chapter we will talk about the various systems on a robot and the various parts needed to build those systems. We'll start with the brain.

All educational robots have a programmable brain of some sort. Whether it's the VEX Cortex, LEGO EV3, or something else, these brains process your programs into commands to make motors move, stop, slow down, reverse, or perform some other action. The brain reads information from sensors, turns on lights, gives us buttons to start and stop programs and access information, and sometimes provides a display screen to give us information. Without a brain, your robot is just a mechanism that you will have to push to get moving. That is because, in most robots, the brain also is connected to the battery and it regulates the flow of power coming from the battery to the motors and sensors. We will refer to the battery/brain combination as the **control system**.

The control system may be integral to the running of your robot, but that doesn't mean it has to be placed in the center. Too often I have seen brains and batteries placed in the top center of a robot just because that's where my students think they have to go. In my class, I have an uphill challenge where students have to build a robot to drive up the steepest ramp possible. They use gears to improve the **torque** (rotational power) of their motors, but they also tend to have a vision of a robot with the brain/battery mounted on top of the motors because that's what the first robot I had them build was like. So that is how they build their uphill climber. In this challenge, having a lower center of

A low center of gravity is key to a robot driving up a steep hill; therefore, things like contollers should be placed on the base of the structure.

gravity is really important, so it would be better to build with the motors on the side and the brain/battery in between them, as low to the ground as possible. That would be best for an uphill climber, but every situation is different. I can't describe each situation for you, but it is important to always consider what the function of your robot will be and then build accordingly. That's what we mean when we say form follows function.

If the control system helps provide the power and instructions to your robot, there must be other systems that are the recipient of the electricity and commands. Most of our robots are mobile, which means they have a wheeled base for movement. We will call this the **mobility system**. (If you are building a stationary robot like a crane, you could refer to this as the **structural foundation**). When we think of a mobility system, we picture movement, which usually means wheels. What causes the wheels to move? The motors do. And how do we increase motor acceleration or torque (speed and power, to keep it simple)? We use gears. And what do we use to connect the wheels to the motors? We can use **shafts**, axles, **bushings**, spacers, washers, and **bearings**. Yes, we can end up using a lot of different parts just to keep our robot moving. And don't forget, wheels are only one way they can move. You can also use tracks to create a robot that moves like a tank, and when you get into advanced robotics, you can always build robots that move without wheels. Before we go there, let's break down the mobility system a bit more:

There are enough pieces at this VEX competition to satisfy the needs and the curiosity of any robot builder.

The basic method of putting together a mobility system is to connect the axles or shafts to the motors or gears and then to the wheels. By itself, the mobility system is not enough for our robot. Technically you could connect and balance your brain and battery on top of your motors, attach some wheels, connect the wires, and start driving, but this is not very practical. Almost all robots have ways of keeping stable and connecting everything together, and we will call this the structural system.

The structural system has two purposes: it connects the control system to the mobility system and keeps the entire robot together in a strong manner. A good structural system will keep the robot from flexing or **bending** at the wrong moment, it will help the robot drive straight and allow all other moveable parts to move smoothly, it may provide attachment or storage points for later use, and—keeping in mind that form follows function—it will be neither too large nor too small but instead just the perfect size to do the job required of it. Almost any of the large structural pieces, along with the multitude of connectors different companies come up with, are part of the structural foundation.

Getting Started

Before I continue any further with systems of a robot and how they all work with each other, I want to stop and give some building tips. Too often in the classroom or on my teams, I have seen students try to attach a motor to a brain, then figure out which wheels or gears to attach to the motor, and then they get lost trying to figure out how to add anything else, like an arm for throwing or sensors of some sort. This is because they have approached the problem backwards, and by connecting the motors directly to the brain, they have created a very inconvenient structural foundation.

The way I suggest you start your build is to first decide what wheels you want to use and then connect those to the motors. Once you have your mobility system, proceed to connect the motors together using structural elements. Finally, when you have your structural foundation and your mobility system in place, add the control system last. The brain and the battery do very little as structural elements. There are only a few considerations for the brain's placement. Usually you have to be able to reach its buttons to stop, start, and choose programs (though with the EV3 iPad app this is not even true anymore). You also may have considerations of weight distribution and center of gravity. Beyond that, the brain just gets in the way. The smooth integration of gears, wheels, and motors with

MINIMIZING MOTORS TIPS

Always accomplish what you can without using extra motors. You only have an allowable amount of motors in each competition, and two of those are almost always used to drive your robot. Minimizing motors is important. So if you can push something by just adding a bumper to the front of your robot, do so. If you can create a catch that falls down when knocked into, but in doing so it drops an arm over a competition module allowing your robot to gain control of it, do so. Sometimes, however, you are going to need to use your motors for more than driving around and bumping into things.

your structure and any other parts you may add is of way more importance than placement of the brain.

What do we have left after control, mobility, and structure? We have two important aspects left to consider on our robots: **actuators** and sensors.

Actuators will allow our robots to manipulate objects, and sensors will provide us with information about the environment to help our robot make decisions. We'll take a look at actuators first.

Actuators

Almost all robotics competitions have similar challenges that, though they vary from year to year thematically and in their details, always require the same underlying actions. Push, pull, throw, pick up, reach up high, and many variations of these are some of the basic actions you will almost certainly need to accomplish. Most of the time, an actuator accomplishes these actions. An actuator in its most basic form is anything that converts energy into motion. Your motors are about as basic an actuator as you can get. They convert electrical energy into motion.

A motor is an actuator, one that converts energy into rotational motion. An exploration of what we can do with rotational motion, beyond turning wheels, should start with the understanding of different motor types. Motor types break down into two major categories: servo and DC. A **DC motor** is a continuous rotation motor that is usually used for high-speed applications, like driving wheels. A protruding shaft sticks out from the motor; it can be attached to gears or wheels. They operate on direct current, and therefore you can easily regulate their speed by regulating current. The other type of motor is the **servo motor**. Servo motors usually are designed to turn 180 degrees: 90 degrees to the left and 90 degrees to the right. It is easy to control the position of a servo motor, though not always as easy to regulate its speed. (I'm speaking in generalities here and of what these motors are designed for; there are always ways to hack or program motors to make them do things other than what they were designed to do.) A servo motor is great if you want to move an arm to a specific position and hold it there.

There is a subcategory of servo motors that are prevalent in robotics and these are called **continuous rotation servos**. A continuous rotation servo is one that is able to spin all the way around and is usually geared internally so that the speed is regulated. EV3 large motors, VEX IQ Smart motors, and VEX Cortex 229 three-wire motors are all examples of continuous rotation servos. Some of these motors also have ways of electronically monitoring the number of rotations and/or degrees they have turned, making them easy to control for duration of turn as well as speed.

Let's look at some practical applications of rotational motion. The simplest type of attachment you can place on a motor is a lever-style arm that is designed to knock or hit something, push down on a lever, push open a door, or other similar action. In this case, a simple long structural piece from whatever type of robot kit you're using can do the trick. This is a good time to use a servo motor. Your arm will probably not spin around and around, and you most likely won't be worried about speed. You will want to be able to control precisely how far down the arm reaches, and you will want to make sure it doesn't turn past its designated point. Arms can, of course, get much more complex than this.

The first level of complexity you can add to this is to have a bucket or some sort of container on top for holding and then dumping/pouring/placing scoring elements in a game. While it is typical to operate this "bucket" with another motor, I challenge you to see if you can operate one without an extra motor. Perhaps the simple action of pushing the bottom of the "bucket" against part of the playing field will cause the top to tip forward and deliver its scoring elements. If you can manage this, you will have saved a motor, and that has several advantages.

Most competitions have limits to the number of motors you are allowed to use. A lot of robotics kits also have a limit to the number of motor ports available. Motors also add extra weight to your robot, they require wiring that can get in the way, and if they are hanging off the end of an arm, they must be secured well or they are prone to break. Still, there are times when you can use several motors to design and build a complex robotic arm.

Degree of Freedom

Take a look at your own arm for a moment. Move it about in as many different ways as you can. Each distinct type of movement is referred to as a **degree of freedom**. My shoulder joint allows me three of these degrees of freedom. I can hold my arm out straight and move it up and down, side to side, and twist it like

Degrees of freedom are what allow this young crossing guard to hold her arms in two very different positions.

I am turning a screwdriver. My elbow adds a fourth degree of freedom and my wrist contributes three more (the same ones as my shoulder) for a total of seven. (I'm excluding the fingers for the sake of simplicity here.) I don't need all of these degrees of freedom to move my hand in any direction, but I do need them to grasp, pick up, and place objects. Go ahead and try picking up items around the room right now and put them in different places. You'll see what I mean. This understanding of human arm movement will inform our building of a robotic arm.

When building a robotic arm, the first question you need to ask yourself is, "How many different ways and places do I need to pick up and drop off an item?" Let's use a common example from my class to help think this through. I will sometimes challenge my students to build a factory assembly line. An item, often a piece of candy, has to make it from one end of the assembly line to another, usually along conveyor belts, while different actions (cutting, painting, drilling) happen along the way. At the end, the student must have an arm pick up the object and move it somewhere else. Working backwards, we can imagine a claw that will have to open and close to grab the object. One degree of freedom and one motor required. We will have to attach that claw to an arm that can lift it up and down so it is not always in the way—a second degree of freedom and a second motor required. Finally, the challenge included moving the block somewhere else. So we need to have a third degree of freedom requiring a third motor to swivel the arm left and right. Remember form follows function? We know what we need to do, so now we know what we need to build.

A complex robotic arm is one of the cooler things you will build taking advantage of the rotational motion of motors. Once you have managed to make a robotic arm, the next step would be to build a **linear actuator**. A linear actuator is anything that converts energy into linear motion, as opposed to rotational. One of the most common types is one that is created mechanically using a **lead screw**.

A lead screw is a long threaded bar turned by a motor. The bar is usually held in place, and a nut of some sort is attached to it so that it moves in a linear fashion along the threads as the motor turns the bar. Usually this nut has threads on the inside but has a larger shape than a regular nut so that you can attach

SHOULDERING THE LOAD

The robotic claw at right was built and programmed with three degrees of freedom to allow it to pick up a blue or white gumball and place it in the appropriate container.

The **color sensor** is held up to the gumball (1) to determine whether it is blue or white. When that determination is made, the middle motor, acting as an elbow, lowers the claw so it can pick up the gumball (2).

Once the claw is over the gumball, the medium motor will close so that the claw captures the gumball. Once it is captured, the elbow motor will lift the arm. A third motor, acting as the third degree of freedom, will turn the entire arm until the claw rests over the tube with the word white written on it (3). Think of this motor as the shoulder of this robotic arm.

Finally, the medium motor—you can think of this as a hand—opens and deposits the gumball (4).

This simple maneuver took three motors. In most competitions, you are limited in the number of motors you are allowed to use, and most robots have a limitation on how many motors you are allowed to attach. Think wisely before you use all of your allowable motors to accomplish one task.

1

2

3

4

things to it. If you ever look at the jack you use to raise your car when changing a flat tire, a lead screw is what makes it rise. Let's now look at one way this linear actuator can be used in our robot.

This jack is being held up by the use of a lead screw, the same mechanism that allows linear actuators to move in our robots.

Along with pushing and pulling, I mentioned that sometimes you might need to lift something up high or reach out a long way past your robot to grab a field module in a competition. In this case, you may need to build something like a **scissor lift**. A scissor lift is a series of paired beams connected in an X fashion, with each pair connected together in their middles and connected to the next pair at their ends. A scissor lift can compact quite small and expand really far while remaining quite sturdy. To raise a scissor lift, you need one of the bottom beams to be pushed in a straight line. That's where a good linear actuator like a lead screw comes in.

There are too many different types of actuators to go into them all in this book. So far we have only described electromechanical ones. These are ones where the energy comes from a battery and turns a motor or uses a mechanism like a lead screw to convert that energy to linear motion. There are linear actuators that use electrical energy but contain the mechanism internally so that you don't have to connect a motor to a lead screw, and there are actuators that use **hydraulics** and pneumatics instead of electricity.

You can purchase a linear actuator for your robot that contains all the parts internally in a long sleeve, with just an extendable arm. In these, the motor itself turns a lead screw that in turn pushes a nut (that is fixed so it doesn't rotate with the screw) horizontally.

If you are ever unsure about how a linear actuator works, take a look at a retractable glue stick, or lip balm, or your roll-on deodorant. All of these push something up in a straight line in response to a turn at the bottom. In other words, they are linear actuators.

There are also linear actuators that are run by pneumatic and hydraulic power. "Pneumatic" refers to any type of compressed gas, but air is the most common. "Hydraulic"

This linear actuator has the screw and nut built internally. The silver "arm" at the end is attached to the nut and is the only part you will see move.

COMPONENTS OF A SCISSOR LIFT

The scissor lift can be compact yet provide long reach. The numbered items below identify the parts of the lift and their functions.

1. Flat platform. Most scissor lifts have a flat top that allows you carry or place items on it.
2. Curved cage. Balls will "shoot" through this upside down U shape and get deposited in the scoring goal.
3. Tension springs. Tension springs are used in a few levels toward the top to keep the scissor lift from wobbling too much.
4. Spring. An ingenious use of the potential energy stored in a cheap plastic spring clamp. As the scissor lift raises, the higher it goes the harder it is to continue. The potential energy in these clamps is turned into kinetic energy as the scissor lift raises and the clamps open.

5. An infrared sensor (shielded) used to detect the infrared transmitter underneath the clear plastic goal on the bottom of the red structure.

6. A DC motor controller. This robot uses an NXT controller, which does not allow for direct control of a DC motor. Usually an extra motor controller is wired to the DC motors and the NXT.

7. NXT controller. This one is decked out in sleek black.

8. Anderson Power Pole connectors. This type of connector for connecting power wires together has become the norm in most robotics applications as it is strong and rarely comes apart.

9. Immobile scissor lift bottom. This left end beam at the bottom of the scissor lift is connected to the bottom of the robot in a manner that holds it stationary.

10. Most robotics competitions require teams to have their team number displayed clearly on two sides of the robot for easy identification by the judges.

11. Linear actuator. This end of the scissor lift is connected to a nut, which in turn is part of a lead screw powered by a DC motor. As the lead screw turns, the nut moves horizontally, thus raising or lowering the scissor lift, depending on the nut's direction.

12. Two NXT motors spin an axle connected to a bunch of black plastic zip ties. These are used to "scoop" up playing elements—wiffle balls—off the floor and into the robot.

13. A chain, most likely operated by a DC motor, is connected to all three wheels on this side of the robot.

14. A plastic boxlike structure surrounds the robot and comes low enough on the wheels so no scoring elements can get under the robot and screw up its mobility.

refers to the use of liquids. In both of these cases, a cylinder and piston are the main components. External pressure is the key to the operation of both of these. An air compressor or some sort of pump increases the pressure on the internal piston, which starts to move and build up the pressure inside the cylinder. As the pressure increases, the cylinder begins to move along the axis of the piston.

Air and Water

Air pressure is easy to control but not very powerful and prone to leakage. For this reason, pneumatic linear actuators are used when precise movement for small loads is needed. Due to the variability in conditions, there are no one-size-fits-all pneumatic linear actuators. Instead, they are made for specific jobs and sold as such. Hydraulic linear actuators, on the other hand, can handle very large loads. This is because liquid is not very compressible. Try squeezing a given volume of water into a smaller space than it naturally occupies. Very difficult indeed!

Pneumatic and hydraulic systems are used in non–linear actuator types of applications as well. LEGO Education produces a very handy pneumatic system, which includes pumps, tubes, pistons of varying sizes, storage containers, and gauges. Look at the robotic hand on the next page that my team made a few years ago. You'll notice there are motors to help mimic the first and second joint of each finger. As cool as this was, it became way too heavy to operate and produce more than a few letters of the American Sign Language alphabet. When they replaced the motors with pneumatic switches operated by air, they were able to decrease the weight a great deal and increase the functionality of the hand.

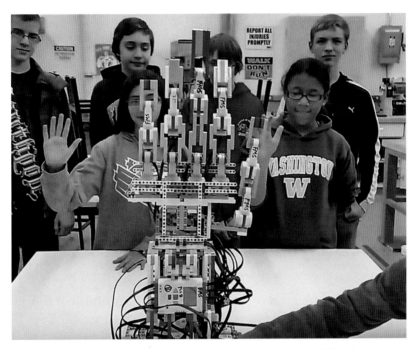

When the Gear Grinders of Graham, Washington, replaced this robotic hand's heavy motors with pneumatics, its functionality was greatly improved.

Sensors

Sensors are the final piece of the puzzle we need in order to complete our understanding of what's in a robot. Simply put, sensors provide the brain of the robot with information about its environment. Sensors don't move or make decisions; they tell the robot what it wants to know, and then the brain makes decisions based on that information.

Sensors are divided into two main categories: analog and digital. An **analog sensor** is one that has an infinite range of values it can return. A **digital sensor** is one that has a discreet range of values. A rotation sensor that measures the amount your motor has turned is an example of an analog sensor. The number of rotations can be infinite and so can the returned value. A **sound sensor** that returns a scaled value between one and one hundred would be a good example of a digital sensor. Whatever type of sensor you're using, it's important to know what it does and does not do.

Sensors are designed for very specific purposes, and if you want your robot to get certain information, you need to make sure you are using the correct sensor to get that information. For example, a color sensor can usually measure different types of light as well as colors. But it can only measure specific colors, or it measures certain types of colors better than others. For one example, the EV3 color sensor can measure **ambient light**, **reflected light**, and color. When you use it, you have to make sure you have selected the correct mode (ambient, reflected, or color) for the information you want to sense.

It is no good trying to follow the reflection of a black line on a white surface if you are using your sensor in color mode. Likewise, you will not be able to distinguish a lot of colors with the EV3 color sensor if you're not reflecting off of LEGO pieces. This sensor is designed to "see" LEGO colors, specifically six of them: red, yellow, green, blue, black, and white, as well as "no color." In my class, I'll often use colored electrical tape to create obstacles and challenges for my students. We've discovered that dark blue usually shows up as black using the color sensor in color mode. This doesn't mean that the color sensor is useless; it just means we have to know how to use it correctly. The same piece of tape will reflect a lower value than a piece of black tape in reflective mode; therefore, reflective is the correct mode to use in this situation.

Let's take a look at some common sensors and their uses.

Jeopardy! *champion Ken Jennings used a touch sensor to indicate when he was ready to answer a question.*

The simplest sensor, and thus the most prevalent sensor in any educational robotics kit, is the **touch sensor**. This digital sensor usually has two conditions: on and off. In other words, it can tell if it has been touched (bumped) or not. With some nifty programming, you can also sense for a touch and release. For example, on the TV trivia show *Jeopardy!*, you are not allowed to click until an answer has been fully read, and you can't hold your thumb on the sensor indefinitely. You have to push it in and release it, and if the person before you provides an incorrect question (in the game show, answers are provided and contestants identify the answer by asking the correct question), you have to wait and click again.

Another common sensor is a sound sensor. This sensor does what it says it does and that is it senses sound. Specifically, most of them sense the total sound in a given area. It would be wrong to think of a sound sensor as a directional microphone. Sound sensors, as do light sensors, usually take a reading and return it in a scaled value for ease of use with programming. For example, the NXT sound sensor takes raw decibel readings that max out at close to ninety and instead returns readings as a percentage of that maximum, so the readout of the sensor would be from 1 percent to 100 percent.

A fun sensor to use and one that elicits a feeling of familiarity due to its design is the distance sensor, also known as an ultrasonic sensor. Most distance sensors send out a signal, usually an ultrasonic frequency, which will bounce back to the sensor when the signal encounters an object. The sensor calculates how long it took for the sound to bounce back and uses that information, along with the speed of the signal, to determine the distance to the object it detected.

The above four sensors (touch, color, ultrasonic, and sound to a lesser extent) are mainstays in most educational robotics kits, along with a one that has gained in popularity recently, the **gyro sensor**. Gyro sensors measure angular velocity around a single axis. For example, if your robot is spinning to the left or right, a gyro sensor can tell you the rate of the turn. By knowing how long you were turning for, the gyro sensor can also tell you the angle of your turn. Or so we would hope.

Since the introduction of gyro sensors to educational robotics, there has been much controversy surrounding their use, their accuracy, and what it is they are actually meant to measure. The determination of angle depends on a lot of factors, including turning at a consistent speed, calibrating the gyro, eliminating the tendency of this sensor to "drift," and a few others. Used correctly and with a bit of practice, the gyro sensor is a powerful tool to add to your robot.

In addition to the ones mentioned above, there are tons more specialty sensors that may not be commonly provided with your robotics kit but are readily available and prevalent. These included some popular ones like **accelerometers**, infrared sensors, and compass sensors, to more esoteric ones used for science experiments like salinity sensors, anemometers (for measuring wind speed), and pH sensors.

Conclusion

Regardless of its type, each sensor is only going to provide you with specific information. In order to get the most out of your sensors, you have to make sure you are using the right sensor for the right information, have it attached in the most advantageous way possible, know how to read it correctly, and program your robot to respond appropriately. In the next chapter, we will take a look at some of these factors, and in chapter 5 we will learn how to effectively program using our sensors.

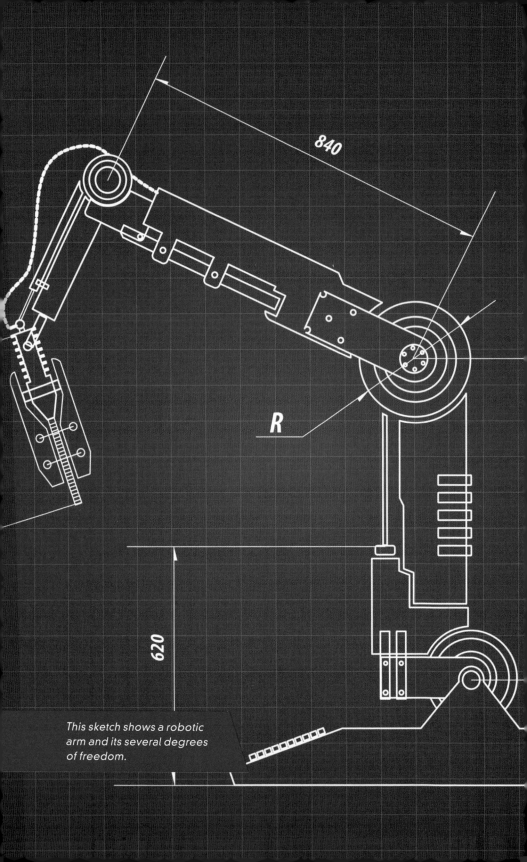

840

R

620

This sketch shows a robotic arm and its several degrees of freedom.

3 Putting It All Together

So now you know how to build a robot, right? Of course you don't. All the theory concerning what a robot is and what the parts are won't really help you when it comes to building a robot. This chapter will lay out some basic guidelines for building, provide you with some strong dos and don'ts, show you some concrete building examples using different products, and provide you with a philosophical approach to use with all your future builds.

One last note before we begin our exploration of how to put parts together: The variations on building are infinite; I cannot possibly show you every way to build a robot, and this book would be impossibly long if I did. Instead, I will show you some sample ideas that illuminate larger concepts. It's up to you, the young engineer, to decide how to apply these concepts to *your* robot.

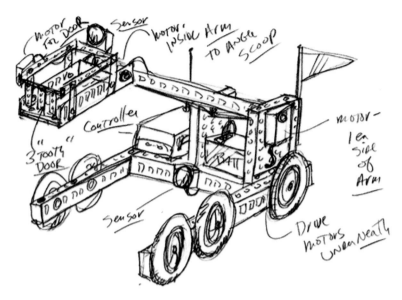

This sketch shows some careful thought went into the design of this FTC robot.

Getting Started

Most engineers have a plan, sketched out in detail, which they follow when they are going to build something. There is a great deal of wisdom in this as it can save you from multiple problems later on. I just finished a mechanical engineering unit with my eighth-grade students. They were tasked with building a child's pull toy that converted the rotational motion of the wheels into some other type of movement. Most students wanted to build right away and gave very short shrift to the required sketches. Two weeks into the project, the number-one comment I heard from students who were struggling to make parts fit together and work was, "I wish I had spent more time sketching out my design," or something to that effect.

While sketching can be very important to help us visualize our ideas and see if they are going to work, I do caution against too much sketching and planning. Before robotics kits were relatively inexpensive and readily available, most designers were building with expensive materials. With LEGO and other products, the entry-level price into robot building is comparatively lower than it used to be. This makes the act of just playing with parts and pieces and putting them together in various configurations an inexpensive activity, which is also an invaluable one.

PART OF THE NAME

To reinforce the belief that playing with pieces is as important as sketching (especially at the beginning stages), look no further than this quote from the LEGO website: "The name 'LEGO' is an abbreviation of the two Danish words *leg godt*, meaning 'play well'. It's our name and it's our ideal."

One of the reasons LEGO has remained a super popular child's toy is because you are always learning with it. When you try to put two pieces together, either they fit or they don't. They might work sort of well or really well. No matter what the outcome is, you have learned something. And because you are actively engaging in the activity of building instead of reading about it, you are way more likely to retain what you learned. We can do this quite easily with VEX IQ or LEGO EV3 pieces. With a kit like Tetrix or VEX EDR, it takes more time to put things together and take them apart;

we're talking snapping and connecting plastic pieces versus screwing hundreds of metal bolts and nuts together. Either way, I encourage you to get out there and play, I mean build, with your pieces.

I don't want you to disavow the value of sketching and planning, but I also don't want you to hesitate before picking up some pieces and seeing if they go together to perform a desired function. The more complex the building material, the more I would suggest doing some heavy planning, which can include sketching, before you start out. The scope of this book is not engineering sketching and design. Topics such as how to shape and cut complex materials and how to use CAD software are covered in the book *Advanced Programming and Design*.

DRAWING TIPS

No one is expecting students to sketch blue print–quality designs. If you're really an unskilled artist, try for clarity of lines and labeling of parts and pieces over realistic depictions and drawings.

Form Follows Function

"Form follows function" means that you have to know what you want your robot to do or accomplish before you start to build it. The way it looks comes after you get it to function the way you want. This doesn't mean that making a cool-looking robot isn't important. It means that it's easier to work on that part after you've gotten all the pieces to work together and do what you want. Your primary goal should be to build a robot that performs the function you want. Even if the form is part of what you are working on, it's always easier to decorate after the functional parts are in place.

For example, in my seventh-grade robotics class in 2016, we worked on a zoo unit. One group attempted a frog that sticks out its tongue when it sees a certain color insect. The group started by building a frog-looking robot and then tried to fit a **rack and pinion** gear (to simulate the tongue) into the mouth area. I told them to take it apart and to work on the tongue first. It's always easier to build around your main mechanism (rack and pinion gear) than to fit that mechanism into your build. We can use this concept of form follows function to start our exploration of building the mobility system in our robot.

Which Wheels and Where?

When building our mobility system, there are many variables to consider. Will your robot need to make tight turns and stop on a dime? Will it drive on flat surfaces or over rough terrain? Does it need to be geared for torque or speed? Do you want to use wheels or tracks? Do you need a specialty wheel like an **omni-wheel**? Do you want small ones or larger ones? The list goes on and on, but it's an important one to consider as we start to build. Let's table these questions for a moment and look at how to attach wheels efficiently.

Wheels turn. Hopefully you knew that. They are usually attached to a shaft or axle that is sometimes turned by a motor. Whatever they are attached to, you want to make sure of a few things: you don't want your wheel to slide off; you don't want it to rub against any part of your robot; and you want the piece it is attached to, to be stable. This last part is extremely important. Take a LEGO axle, for example. It is designed to fit through the holes on a beam. But if you place it through one beam only, the fact that it can fit through that beam also means there is room for it to wiggle, and this is not good. Instead, you should place that axle through a minimum of two beams.

WHEEL STABILITY TIP

The further away the wheel is from the beam the axle goes through, the greater the lever effect is going to increase the lack of stability in your axle.

Wheels

For the majority of competition robotics, as well as for a lot of the classroom applications I have seen, wheeled robots are used. So how do we decide which wheels to use? If you're expecting me to write form follows function, you're correct. What do you want to do with those wheels? Again, the answers to this question can be infinite, but we can look at some generalizations to help us get started.

The number-one question students ask me when they are working on my gear challenge (to build an uphill climber or a drag racer) is, "Are bigger or smaller wheels faster?" The quick answer is that big wheels will turn faster. To demonstrate this I conduct an experiment with my students. On a sunny day, I take them outside and draw three concentric circles on the pavement with chalk. One is about 3 feet (0.9 meters) in diameter, one is 10 feet (3 m), and the diameter of the third is 20 feet (6 m). I place a student on each circle so that they are in line with each other. I tell them that when I say go, they all need to move around their circle in a clockwise direction so that they arrive back at their starting point at the same time. If you are picturing this in your mind, I am sure you can guess what happened. The student in the 10-foot diameter circle has to start jogging to catch up with the student walking the 3-foot diameter, and the one on the outermost (20-foot diameter) circle has to run fast to have any chance at all of making it back at the same time as the others.

To stay even with the other runners on a curve, the outside competitor must move faster because he has farther to go.

Don't run away now thinking that bigger equals faster and that's all there is to it. As a matter of fact, there is a lot more to it, specifically if you are looking to create a fast-moving robot like a drag racer. Before it zooms down a racetrack, your robot

AXLE DOS AND DON'TS

Two EV3 motors with the same wheel and gears, set up differently.

The above EV3 motor setups appear the same, but they are actually quite different. The one on the left has several common mistakes. The axle is only supported by one beam. This leaves wiggle room. The axle itself is much longer than needed, and the wheel is too far from the structure that supports it. The motor on the right uses two beams, providing more stability for the axle. The wheel is much closer to the beam, and though it's hard to see, there is a bushing keeping the wheel from rubbing against the beam. By placing the same-sized bushing on the right wheel's setup, you will have assured yourself of a symmetrical wheelbase for your robot, which is very important for making accurate turns.

A wheel and motor on VEX EDR set up using good building practices.

The above photo shows a strong motor-to-wheel connection using VEX EDR pieces. The shaft runs through two supporting pieces, minimizing wiggle. The wheel is kept on the shaft using a metal shaft collar with a setscrew. Spacers are used so there is not room for the wheel to slide. Bearings are also provided so the shaft can turn smoothly. Shafts are square, and so are the holes in VEX metal pieces. The edges of the shaft are rounded, but they still rattle if they are just spinning through metal, so the rule is whenever a metal shaft goes through a hole, you should use a bearing for smooth turning. Finally, a rubber shaft collar is used on the inside of the shaft, close to the motor, to add more security against slipping.

must overcome **inertia**. Inertia is the tendency of a body to resist a change in its motion. If something is moving, it will keep moving until a force acts upon it, and if it is resting, it will not move until another force acts upon it. The more mass an object has, the greater its resistance to a change in its motion. Therefore a heavier object will be more difficult to move than a lighter one.

So what does this have to do with our wheels? Besides the fact that larger wheels usually have a larger mass than smaller wheels, there is also a concept referred to as moment of inertia. I am simplifying physics here, but we can think of moment of inertia as the inertia of an object that rotates around an axis (like a wheel) rather than the inertia of an object traveling in a straight line (like a robot). The moment of inertia increases greatly as the distance from the axis increases, meaning the larger the diameter of the wheel, the larger the moment of inertia. Therefore, while the outside of a larger wheel will turn faster than the outside of a smaller one (if both are connected to motors turning at the same speed), a greater force will also be needed to make it overcome its inertia before it can reach full speed.

This is not to be taken as a prohibition against using large wheels when speed is the desired outcome. It is instead a warning to consider all aspects of using wheels before you're too quick to choose one type over another.

Types of Turns

The next major consideration we're going to look at is how to choose wheels to make our robots turn. When you think of a car turning, it's a steering wheel that causes the two front wheels to angle themselves in order to make a turn. The wheels use a rack and pinion gear to enable them to turn. While I have seen some robots emulate this sort of steering mechanism, it's not very common. Instead, the usual method to turn a robot is to use the speed and direction of the wheels on each side.

SPINNING YOUR WHEELS

In order for a point turn to work properly, the wheels must be equidistant from the center of the robot.

You can make two different types of turns this way: a swing turn and a point turn. A swing turn happens when the wheel(s) on one side of the robot turn more than on the other. If one side is simply moving faster than the other, the robot will tend to drive forward in either a left or right curving motion. If one side doesn't move at all, the robot will tend to pivot around the non-turning side. In other words, if my right motor turns my wheels, and my left motor doesn't move, my robot will turn to the left, pivoting around the wheels on the left side. In a point turn, the wheels on one side will turn forward, while the wheels on the other side will be spun backward by their motor, both at the same speed. This will cause the robot to spin in place around its center. This type of turn is nice if you don't have a lot of room in which to maneuver. With either of these types of turns, we run into a problem. If our robot is turning and our wheels are in a forward fixed position, then our wheels must be sliding across the surface they are driving on. And if they have rubber tires, the friction created by the rubber can cause a jerking motion as the wheels slide.

This slippage can be a major cause of frustration to team members when competing. I have seen my own team become really upset when its robot doesn't turn exactly the same way in a competition as the way it did in practice. There are a few ways to overcome this tendency of the wheels to slip. The first one is to take tires off the back wheels (if you're using front-wheel drive) and allow them to slide but decrease the friction so that your robot doesn't bump and jump as it slides. You can imagine that this method is not ideal. Another option is to use four-wheel drive. While this tends to lessen the slippage of wheels during a turn, it doesn't eliminate it, and there are some other disadvantages to using four-wheel drive. The other two options involve the use of special types of wheels.

One common wheel that has gained popularity in recent years is the omni-wheel. An omni-wheel is one

The green rollers on this omni-wheel allow it to move in a direction that is 90 degrees to its main axis of rotation.

that is multidirectional. In most cases, though types differ quite drastically, rollers, which spin perpendicular to the main direction of rotation of the wheel, are placed in two intermittent rows around the circumference of the wheel. They are also spaced at intervals so that at any given moment one roller is making contact with the ground in order to provide lateral movement, while the other side of the wheels is able to make contact for forward movement.

Structural System

The development of the structural system of your robot will differ based on what products you are building with. Some products like EV3 have motors that can become part of the structural system of your robot. Others, like Tetrix, have motors that simply have a shaft protruding from them and require you to build the structural parts separately before attaching the motors or the wheels.

Remember, form will always follow function, so the build and purpose of our structural system will depend on what type of robot we want to make. If we're building a construction crane, our structural system will include a solid place for our controller, connection points for motors that move the various parts of the crane, and the boom and counterweight. If we are building a mobile robot for a competition, then our structural system is going to provide a connection point for the motors and wheels, a base for the controller, mounting areas for various manipulators, and solid connection points for any sensors we are going to use.

Regardless of what type of structural system we are going to build, there are several important concepts to follow that will help make your structure sound, strong, and efficient. The first of these is to use **cross bracing**.

Cross bracing is a method of reinforcing horizontal and vertical supports with pieces that cross perpendicularly or at some other angle. Think of the triangular trusses you see in a bridge. That is a form of cross bracing. To understand why cross bracing is so important, we have to first take a look at the basic square structure that most of us build and what the weak points of that structure are.

While more and more companies are making pieces that allow angular connections, we still end up with a lot of 90-degree angles when we build robots, and this leads to a lot of squares and rectangles. There is nothing wrong with starting our builds this way; we just have to be aware of the weaknesses associated with this type of structure and how to use our building materials and strategies to counter them. The different forces we have to look out for are **shear, tension,** and **compression**.

Shear, tension, and compression are three of the most common types of forces that can break things. The other two forces, which are combinations of the first three, are called **torsion** and bending. Compression is when forces are applied directly opposite each other, one pushing down and one pushing up (the force pushing up can come from the surface that is supporting the object being compressed). If two pulling forces are being applied in opposite directions, directly opposite each other, this is called tension. Tuning a guitar puts tension

If this musician turns the tuning peg on the guitar too far, the tension will cause the string to snap.

on a string, which will snap if too much tension is applied. Shear is when two forces, not in direct opposition, are pulling something apart.

These are the three main forces that will act upon our robots, either on individual pieces, on structures, or on the entire robot. It all depends on the specific situation, and we can't possibly account for all of them in one book. The forces applied in a typical robotics competition usually won't involve bending, but it's important to understand what it is.

Bending is a combination of compression and tension. The overloaded bookshelf that is bowing is a classic example of bending. The middle of the shelf, where you usually see it bowing, is reacting to a compressing force that is pushing molecules inside the board together. The bottom of the board is in tension and is pulling apart under the force. Most structures in reaction to a bending force will break on the bottom part that is in tension.

The last force, torsion, is not often seen in the types of robotics applications we will be using at the high school level but is important to understand as it may occur at some point. Think of torsion as a twisting force. When I was young, my sister and I used to "play" by grabbing the other's forearm in both hands and twisting in opposite directions, causing a burning sensation. Kids, huh? This twisting force is called a torsional force. If the force were strong enough to break bones (thankfully it wasn't), the inside of the bones would shear apart.

The question is: How do we build structures that resist these forces, especially if, at any given point, we aren't sure which ones may be applied to our robots? Structures utilizing 90-degree angles in their builds are susceptible to one or more of these forces, so we're going to apply cross bracing to our structures.

Whichever kit you're using and whatever competition you may be competing in, the materials used are often proportional to the expected forces that may be applied to them. For example, most of the robots you see built out of LEGO pieces are nowhere near large or strong enough to withstand the compressive forces of more than a few pounds. Because of this, a competition like FIRST LEGO League won't require you to move or lift anything too heavy. But if you've been around robots a long time, you will have seen a lot of them break and fail under forces they should be able to withstand. This is because the failure points are usually the connection points, which are usually located in the corners where two or more pieces meet. By applying cross bracing you can reinforce your structures by adding new points of contact to withstand shearing and tension forces.

There are two types of cross bracing: vertical and diagonal. Vertical cross bracing will resist compression but only at the center point where it meets the main structure. It provides a point at the center, which resists any bending forces and also transmits any shearing or tensile forces along the entire structure and not just at the corners.

Diagonal cross bracing is even stronger than vertical cross bracing in that it resists shearing and tensile forces while also transmitting a compressive force to the whole structure rather than just the points at which the compression occurs.

Compression has caused the LEGO square (top left) *to fail at its connection points* (top right). *Adding support by right-angle beams* (bottom left) *and by diagonal cross-bracing* (bottom right) *resists compression.*

The trusses in a bridge do the same thing; they are diagonal cross braces, which transmit force along the entire structure. Whether you apply diagonal or vertical cross bracing depends on what type of forces you are building your robot to withstand. Of the two, diagonal is stronger but more difficult to build as the attachment points of most of our robots are designed for 90-degree connections. However as you move up in complexity in the robotics world, you will find the need (and in upper-level competitions, the freedom) to drill holes anywhere you like to apply just the right piece in just the right place.

Diagonal cross bracing connected in the center helps support a heavy arm motor on top of this structure.

Sometimes we can't find the space to use cross bracing, or it will get in the way of some other part of our robot. In these cases, we need to make sure we are taking advantage of all the other building options we have that can reinforce the strength of our robot. It sounds simple, but the first thing to make sure of is that whenever we are connecting two pieces together, we connect them with at least two connections. This means beams in LEGO overlap beams and have at least two pins connecting them. In other applications where you're using nuts and bolts, always use two instead of one. The reason for this is simple:

two metal beams have the ability to pivot around a single contact point; when you add a second point, you eliminate this ability. And when you're attaching pieces, there are often ready-made parts and pieces that allow you to make connections that resist the forces of tension, shear, and compression. Take advantage of these to create strong structures. Keep in mind which type of force(s) you are most likely to encounter and build accordingly.

Actuators and Manipulation

Manipulation of objects by a robot is essential. Most of the time, manipulation is accomplished by the use of an actuator, which is something that converts energy into motion. I say most of the time because there are a few times when it is easier to use the entire robot to manipulate an object. For example, in 2010 the FIRST Tech Challenge included a scoring element in which you had to move a bowling ball up a ramp and deposit it in a hole at the top. My team built a tall robot that had a gap in the front large enough for a bowling ball. We would drive over the bowling ball, then capture it inside the robot and drive it up the ramp. In this way, we turned our entire robot into a manipulator and saved the energy, motors, pieces, and parts that an arm or lifting mechanism would have required for something else. This was a great solution, but there are times when it won't work and you will have to build a type of actuator in order to manipulate an object.

The simplest type of an actuator is probably an arm, which is usually a beam of some sort attached to a gear or wheel. As a motor turns the gear, the arm lifts up and down or left to right, cutting an arc through the air. The longer an arm you use on your robot, the more leverage the end of it is going to have. This can lead to an arm "slipping" back down from a desired position, either with a heavy object on its end or as it is reaching for something. Programmatically, there are some solutions for positional accuracy of your arm, as well as some motors, like a 180-degree servo, that hold their position quite well. There are also some really good ways to improve this type of actuator using a worm drive mechanism.

A worm drive mechanism is comprised of two parts: the worm, which is a gear that has the appearance of screw threads along a shaft, and the worm gear, which is similar in appearance to a spur gear. The worm turns the worm gear and provides a large increase in torque, so large in fact that the worm gear cannot turn the worm; the mechanism only

A worm turns a worm gear, but force on the worm gear will never be able to turn the worm.

works in one direction. It is for this reason that a worm drive is useful for a lift arm. While a motor can turn the worm, and the worm can turn the worm gear, the worm gear itself will hold its position, even when confronted with a heavy load. The worm gear (and anything attached to it, like an arm) cannot turn the worm. Only when the motor reverses will the worm drive mechanism turn in the opposite direction. And the large increase in torque also means a reduction in speed, so there is very little chance of overshooting your mark.

Other Popular Mechanisms for Manipulation

We have already looked at a few of the other mechanisms available to us. For lifting things high, a scissor lift is quite useful. In a scissor lift, you use a linear actuator to push a beam horizontally. This beam is connected in its middle to another beam that is held stationary. Together they form an X. The ends of the X are connected to another pair of beams, and so forth. The opening and closing of these beams look like a pair of scissors.

Don't forget a linear actuator on its own can be useful for pushing, throwing, or shooting something. You can create one with a rack and pinion, make one using pneumatics or hydraulics, use a lead screw or even a cam and follower (though this provides limited range and will be reciprocating), or a number of other ways.

A forklift can be used when you need to get something off of the floor. A forklift can be created using pulleys and belts, a lead screw placed vertically, or by turning a conveyor belt vertically and moving it over small distances.

If throwing things over a long distance is your goal, do not discount the use of rubber bands or other elastic material. They can be launched with speed and accuracy sometimes greater than that of the motor that releases them. This is because of their elastic property and stored kinetic energy. As long as they are held in place by some type of arm attached to a motor, when the motor releases the arm, the elastic will snap and your object will be launched. Check rules of competitions carefully; some do not allow you to pull back a rubber band or pump up a pneumatic tank beforehand and some do. You have to know the rules.

Sensor System

The sensor system is comprised of very few pieces. Basically these are the sensors themselves and whatever hardware you are using to attach them to the robot. For a complete list of sensors and specifics on how to attach them, please reference my book *Sensors and the Environment.* For the purposes of this chapter, I will cover the most important considerations when building with the more popular sensors.

Sensors need to be attached where they are going to be able to give you the information you are looking for. If you are looking for how far away a 1-foot (30-centimeter) tower is from your robot, it does no good to place your ultrasonic sensor 1.5 feet (45 cm) off the ground. An ultrasonic sensor is going to work best when the signal that is being sent hits the object whose distance you are measuring at a 0-degree angle. This will give you the best opportunity to have the high frequency wave bounce directly back to you and give you the best reading possible.

Interference is another issue you have to consider when thinking about placing sensors. Wires can interfere with sensor readings, and this is especially true of the aforementioned ultrasonic sensors. Keep the wires tucked out of the way behind the sensors themselves. Although you'll rarely encounter this in indoor competitions, sunlight and/or flames can wreak havoc with the readings on an infrared sensor. Sound sensors can be affected by the sound of the motors, and compass sensors can be affected by the magnetic field created by motors and by wires carrying high voltage. It's usually a good idea to mount a compass sensor on the top of a vertical beam, away from wires and motors.

TEST BEFORE ATTACHING

Be aware of the chance of interference with your sensors and test your readings before you attach sensors in a way that makes them hard to remove or adjust.

There are as many types of interference out there as there are sensors. Here is an example of a lesson learned by my FIRST Tech Challenge (FTC) team in 2016. For the 2015–2016 competition season, FTC totally changed the hardware and software rules. Gone was the use of a LEGO NXT programmed by RobotC, and in its place was the use of two Android smartphones programmed by MIT App Inventor: one on the robot sending signals to motors and reading signals from sensors, and one plugged into your game controller for the driver-operated portion of the competition. My team built a cool-looking robot with a sturdy setup for their phone, motor controller, and sensor controller modules. All three of these were connected to each other and were mounted in the top center of the robot. Of course, this meant that they had metal framing pieces above, below, and to the sides of them. In this sense, we had created a **Faraday cage**.

A Faraday cage is a type of enclosure, consisting of conductive materials (like metal), that tends to block certain types of signals, like those coming wirelessly from a phone. Though technically not a sensor, you can see how this type of interference could give you very inaccurate sensor readings. You want to be really careful about where you place your sensors.

The voltage does not hurt the woman in this picture because a Faraday cage is protecting her.

You also want to be careful about how to attach them. A sensor needs to be secure, so that it doesn't move around at all in relation to the robot. Your readings won't be valid if your sensor is shaking or moving. As we've said earlier, sensors need to be free from interference. Sensors also need to be close enough to the phenomena they're sensing to give you accurate readings. I've seen this latter mistake made often when it comes to the use of color sensors.

Color sensors, which can usually detect colors or reflective light depending on their mode, will give you differing readings depending on how close you are to the item you're sensing. As you move away from the item, the reflection off that item gets diffused and your readings will be lower, thus making it hard to distinguish one item from another. Almost all color sensors in their color mode need to be really close, about 0.5 inches (1.25 cm) from the colors they're reading. Otherwise they usually return a value of black. Make sure you find out how close you have to be to an item to get a useful reading before mounting the sensor. I have often seen teams place a color sensor on their robot and then see what readings they get. If they don't get useful ones, they give up on the color sensor. This is not the right way to go about it. Find out where it needs to be first and build accordingly. Form follows function.

The Control System

You may wonder why I didn't discuss the control system first. After all, it's the brain and power of the robot. It's what executes programs, sending signals to motors and reading information from sensors. Without it, we have a pretty mechanism that needs to be pushed. I am writing about the control system last because the decision of where to put it should come last.

With the case of products like VEX IQ and LEGO EV3, the brain seems to be an integral building part of the entire robot. This shouldn't always be the case though. My students discover this quickly when building their drag racers. They try to build the whole thing around the EV3 brick, and more often than not, they fail. When I tell them to build solid motors with gears and wheels and then attach them together with solid framing pieces and *only after* all that add the brick, it's like a lightbulb goes off in their brains. Unfortunately, because most students build robots by following instructions that have the brick as the center, it's how they become oriented to building. It's important to break that habit early. This is easier to do with more advanced building systems.

In the case of a product like VEX EDR or the FTC bots I mentioned, the control system is something that has to be attached; it's not designed to be an integral part of the overall build.

Since we are not making these the centerpiece of our robots that we are going to build around, what do we need to consider? The wires from your motors and sensors (or motor and sensor controllers) are going to go to your brain, so you have to place it somewhere those wires can reach. It can't interfere with the operation of the motors, wheels, arms, actuators, etc. It needs to be easy to reach for plugging in wires, turning on and off, and downloading new programs.

You wouldn't want to make this delicate module the center of your robot's chassis.

And finally, it should be attached so that it can withstand the vibrations of a moving robot. My same FTC team that created a Faraday cage with their first robot ran into a new problem with their redesign. They placed their Android phone (control system) up high so it wouldn't have any signals blocked. They also attached it so the micro USB plug that went into its side was stressed and could be pulled out from the force of gravity. They lost their connection to their motors several times this way, and their robot stopped responding in the middle of competition rounds. Live and learn.

Conclusion

By now, you know what a robot is, what it does, and how to put one together. In the final two chapters, we will look at how to think like a robot and how builders and programmers solve problems. Finally, we'll learn how to program robots to truly turn them into useful tools instead of just lumps of plastic and metal.

This bomb-detecting robot has an advantage over humans doing the job; there are no emotions to rattle or scare it.

4 Problem-Solving People and Robots

I have spent more than a decade teaching and coaching robotics. In that time, I have encountered numerous problems, and every time I thought I overcame one, a new one popped up to take its place. So while I don't have all the answers by any stretch of the imagination, I do have a number of solid strategies that can help you build and program a successful robot or become a member of a winning robotics team.

Top Ten Troubleshooting Tips

Before I go into any lengthy explanation of how to solve major problems with your robot, let me first supply you with the some simple solutions to common robot problems.

1. You keep running the program over and over and it's not working right. I wrote about this one first because it is one of the most common among my students. To fix this, make sure that you are running the correct program. Often times students will get lazy with their nomenclature, allowing default names like "Program1" and "Program2" to be used instead of assigning descriptive names like "DragRace." By not using descriptive names and allowing the program to assign default names, you are running the risk of forgetting which program is the correct and accurate one, especially when working on a project for a period of a few weeks or more.

2. You ran the program, but only one motor turns, and only for a brief second. Check the wires. One is probably loose and not securely plugged into either the motor or motor port. What is actually happening is the robot brain has sent electricity out along its wires to the motors. As soon as one of these motors (the unplugged one) doesn't send an electrical pulse back, the brain shuts the motors down.

3. You have an arm that is stuck and the robot won't complete the next command in your program. The motor that controls the arm that got stuck was probably programmed for using degrees or rotations for its duration. It is still trying to execute its command and won't go on to the next command until this one is complete. Try using seconds instead. The motor will turn for the stated time duration and then stop, allowing the program to progress to the next command.

4. Your robot is not sensing something even though it is clearly there and you can see it with your own two eyes. Check your ports. Oftentimes the port that a sensor is plugged into and the port that you are trying to control in your program are not the same. This can happen with motors as well. Most robotics software programs now use some form of **auto-identification**

for their motors and sensors, so this is becoming less of a problem, but I still encounter it often among my students.

5. You programmed your motors to turn on and thought that would make your robot run forever. Instead it stopped after just making the feeblest of efforts to move. What you need to understand is that programming is sequential. A program will execute a command, then immediately after, it will look for the next command to execute. If there are no more commands, then the robot will stop; it will assume the program is done and there is nothing left to do. That is why we always program our robots to run for a certain duration of time or distance (motor degrees/rotations) or until a sensor senses something.

6. You know the color that your sensor is supposed to tell you a certain item is. You've even held up the sensor to the item several times and checked. But when you run the program you get a different reading. The problem here is a common one that can be applied to many things, not just the color sensor. When you held up the sensor to your item (let's say a gumball), you probably held it close enough and still enough until you got an accurate reading. A yellow gumball showed up as yellow, for example. But when you run your gumball-sorting program, yellow shows up as something else. That's because the conditions aren't the same. The distance of the gumball from the color sensor in your robot is different than when you held the sensor next to it to get your accurate reading, and the same is true for the speed with which the gumball might pass your sensor. Always test sensors under the actual conditions they'll work with when the robot is running.

7. Your robot veers to the right/left. This single problem is probably the bane of more FIRST LEGO League teams than any other. There are a number of reasons why this may be happening. First, check to see that the drive wheels are equidistant from the center of the robot. Both wheels should be exactly the same distance away from the motors that drive them. Perhaps an asymmetrical build or a heavy load is causing drag on one side of the robot. Check your axles. As was mentioned in chapter 3, torsion can cause axles to twist, and this will not allow them to turn properly. You may also want to check for bent axles. What about your back wheels? Are you using a castor wheel like those supplied with the EV3? These can get dirty quickly and cause problems for straight driving. Are any tires rubbing against the motors? You should use some sort of spacer or bushing to keep your tires from rubbing.

8. Your motors are running at different speeds. More often than not, this is a figment of the imagination. It just seems like your motors are different. But sometimes it is true. There's an easy way to check and to deal with this problem. You can connect two motors by placing an axle through both of them. Run the motors at the same time. After about ten seconds, if the motors are still in sync, then you're OK. But if you notice that one of the motors starts to bounce off the table, then you have two motors that are running at slightly different speeds. Repeat the experiment with as many motors as you can find until you get two that stay together for the longest period of time.

9. Your wheels seem wobbly. This is similar to number 7 but might not cause you to veer one way or the other; instead your robot just "bounces" as it rides. Check the tires. Tires should be seated in the rim of your wheel, or at least be aligned with the wheel. Sometimes tires slip out of the rim or become unaligned. This can cause some seriously bad driving.

10. Your robot keeps turning off or the Bluetooth connection is not working. I mention these two seemingly disparate problems because the same thing often causes them both: low battery power. The power in most robots is regulated so the motors will still turn at full power even while the battery is at half power, so it's hard to use motor performance as an indicator of battery power. But I have found that Bluetooth performance with the LEGO EV3 is something that fails quite quickly when a robot is out of power. And they also have a tendency to turn themselves off, which makes sense since you don't want them to completely die on you. So please check your battery levels every time you use your robot.

Think Like a Robot

If I asked you to bang your fist on the table until it hurt unbearably, I doubt that any of you would do it. It takes a great deal of will power and self-control to force you to hurt yourself. For a robot, it takes nothing but a command. This is the fundamental difference between you and a robot: a robot will respond to any command given to it, even if those commands break the robot or cause it to drive into a wall or off a cliff. It will do these things gladly and happily (if you program it to display a smile).

Engineers working on anthropomorphic robots are starting to create programming **algorithms** that allow robots to distinguish between commands that are safe and those which may cause harm, but this endeavor is in its infancy, and the desired behavior to choose a safe path must still be programmed. When we work with our robots, they're probably not going to drive off cliffs like lemmings or attack us without warning, but more often than not they are going to drive into walls, throw things the wrong way, drive off a table, or do something else that causes damage and frustrates students.

In order to stop (or at least limit) this type of behavior, we must learn to think like a robot. Let's start with self-preservation. A robot has absolutely no sense of self-preservation. You won't willingly walk into a wall, but a robot will drive right into one, and the motors will keep turning until you pick it up and turn it off. Here's what you do in this situation: Walk, see wall, know it's a bad idea to walk into it, stop. We can program our robot to drive forward, we can program it to sense an object a certain distance away, and we can program it to stop. But we have to give it these commands. We can't just assume it will stop after it sees a wall just because that's what you or I would do.

When you want a robot to follow a command when it senses something, you need to tell it to do so. I call this the Rule of Three: Do something, sense something, do something else. It's this last part that students often forget to program. Every year, I know I will have a number of bright-eyed students staring at their program, wondering why their robot is driving into a wall. Nine times out of ten, I know why. When I look at their

Nobody programmed this drag racer to stop at the end of the race, so it just kept going right up the wall.

program, I notice they have the robot driving forward, they have it looking for an object that is 8 inches (20 cm) away, but they forget to tell it what to do when it sees that object. This is because they have forgotten to think like a robot and aren't applying the Rule of Three. In their minds, they are thinking that if they see a wall they would stop; but if their robot sees the wall, it doesn't know to stop unless you tell it to do so.

I will elaborate on how to apply the Rule of Three in the next chapter. For now, understand that it works for most basic actions where sensors are involved. Drive forward, use the color sensor to sense a line, then you must also tell the robot to stop on the line, turn, or execute some other action.

Teamwork

Unless you've picked up a robot on your own and are programming it at home, you have been most likely placed with a team or at least a partner, and this may or may not be to your liking. Nothing is more important than forming a good working relationship with these people. I have seen teams that are supportive and work beautifully together achieve way more than the sum of their parts; but I have never seen a team full of individual genius builders and programmers get very far if they can't work together or get along at all. So how do you do that?

This isn't a book on the psychology of team building; I do, however, have three simple suggestions when it comes to working with people that you may not know well or get along with at the beginning. The first is to listen more than you speak. The second is to test ideas rather than argue about them. And the third is to forget about robotics and go bowling. Seriously. Let's examine these one at a time.

Students (and sometimes their coaches/teachers) are really quick to tout their idea about a robot or to jump on somebody else's idea and put it down. Instead, try listening. Listen all the way until everyone has had a turn to speak. Speak when it's your turn, not before. When everybody's had a chance to speak, then you can try to build a consensus around ideas and offer constructive criticism. If a team member or partner has a critique of your idea, listen. Don't argue or fight. Oftentimes we take ownership of our ideas, we get upset when people attack them, and we get very heated in their defense. You have to let this feeling go and be willing to listen to other people, especially if you want them to listen to you. Remember, in the end it's not *your* robot; it's your team's robot.

Being that it is your team's robot, you want to build one that is successful. Instead of getting into an argument about whose idea is better, test them all out. Let's say one half of the team

Taking a break from building to watch a funny video on your phone can be just the thing to shed the stress of arguing about the robot.

wants to use tank tracks to get over a certain obstacle, while the other half of the team thinks omni-wheels are the way to go for faster movement and accurate turns. They can't both be right, can they? Well actually they can. The tracks might help you at certain points in a competition, while the omni-wheels will help you at a different part. The only way to know for sure is to try both and see which one is more successful, which one gives you the most points in all situations (turning and obstacles). It's OK if your idea is not the more successful one; it's still your robot. You're still on the team that came up with the winning design, and that is what matters in the end.

Go bowling. Or play video games. Or take a few selfies together before class starts (and the teacher catches you using your phone in school). You don't have to become lifelong friends with the person you were partnered with in class or the students who showed up after school to join the robotics team. But you will have to have a working relationship with them. Often this can be accomplished by allowing yourselves to have a bit of fun. Whether it's a thirty-second funny video on YouTube before class or a pizza party with the team, these breaks from the robot can prove refreshing and remind you that you are all human beings. Some things are just not worth fighting about, but if you see your partner as a person first, it's easier to remember that in the heat of the moment.

How Far Should We Go?

One of the most common problems to solve in robotics is to know how far to program our robots' motors and wheels to go for in order to reach a certain objective. It also illustrates how you can use math to solve problems. Oftentimes you can't use a sensor or sensors to tell you when you've reached your destination, and you'll have to rely on other methods. Luckily, the circular nature of our wheels gives us a great tool to use in determining how far we need to program our robots to go.

How do you suppose most robots like the *Spirit Rover* (a NASA robot that drives around Mars and studies the planet) know how far they've gone? How do they calculate the distance they've traveled? An advanced robot like *Spirit*, built by some of the top scientists in the United States, will have many sensors that help it identify its location and how far it's traveled, but it will always come back to one basic method: calculating distance using wheel circumference.

Most robots have wheel encoders that tell you how many times a wheel has traveled, either in degrees or rotations. As long as you know the diameter of your wheel, you can use this information together with the number of rotations to accurately

The Spirit Rover *on Mars uses known information such as its wheel circumference and rotations to calculate distance traveled.*

calculate distance traveled. Of course you'll need our friend pi to do this.

Pi is an approximation of the relationship between the diameter of a circle and the circle's circumference. The circumference is the distance around the circle. If you know the distance around your wheel and how many times your wheel has rotated, you need to multiply these two numbers together to determine how far you've traveled. All you need to know is how to calculate circumference.

Circumference is calculated by multiplying the diameter of a circle (in this case, your robot's wheel) times pi. Pi is an irrational number that goes on (so far as we know) infinitely. But for most common applications, engineers use the approximation of 3.14. If you multiply 3.14 by the diameter of your wheel, you will arrive at the circumference, the distance around. And after calculating the circumference, you just multiply it by the number of rotations to get the distance traveled.

In order to prove this works to my students, I set up a simple challenge. On the end of the tables in my room I place different Star Wars bobbleheads. (Hey, I'm a robotics teacher who writes books about robots. Do you really think I don't own Star Wars bobbleheads?) These are placed right at the very edge of the table, with the challenge being to knock them off without having your robot drive off the edge of the table. But there's a catch.

On the table I have used black electrical tape to create three different lines representing three different distances to the bobbleheads. My students must run their robots starting from behind each of these three lines. The catch is they're supposed to try and get the programming right the first time, no trial and error. And to do this, they must use math. Specifically, they need to follow these steps: (1) measure diameter; (2) calculate circumference by multiplying the diameter times pi; (3) measure the distance from the line to the bobblehead; (4) divide the overall distance by the circumference. The answer is the number of rotations you need to program your robot to drive forward from that line to knock a bobblehead off the edge of the table.

To make an abstract concept concrete, let's use the large black tire from the LEGO EV3 expansion set and a piece of tape making a line 66 centimeters (26 inches) from the edge of the table. This tire measures 6.9 centimeters (2.7 inches) across, meaning it has a diameter of 6.9 centimeters. Multiplying that by pi (3.14), my calculated circumference is 21.67 centimeters (8.53 inches). If the line I am starting from is 66 centimeters away from the edge of the table, then I need to divide 66 by

21.67, which gives me an answer of 3.05. That means I have to program my robot to drive 3.05 rotations in order for it to drive from the line right up to the edge of the table. When done right, the results look like this:

Correct programming will get you right where you need to be, and no farther.

How Do You Do That?

Your team's working together really well, you have a great grasp of the parts of a robot and how they go together, and you know a bunch of tips and tricks to help you troubleshoot your robot. What do you do now to put it all together and create a working robot that accomplishes a task?

First, you need to clearly know what goal you are trying to accomplish. Second, you need to break down this goal into manageable chunks that may include programming and building. Third, you may want to break each of those parts down into even more manageable chunks which individuals or small groups can work on. And at each step along the way, you want to stay in communication with the other members to make sure all your individual efforts are going to fit together into a cohesive whole.

I want to illustrate this process by using a concrete example. Let's take a look at the Roomba robot vacuum cleaners. Since iRobot, the producers of the Roomba, released their first model in 2002, these little guys have amazed and astounded onlookers, and while they haven't replaced the hand-held vacuum cleaner in everybody's home, they have come a long way in the last decade from items of curiosity to the main floor-cleaning device in many a home. Since their founding, they have sold more than fifteen million units, according to the 2015 iRobot Annual Report.

So how do you make a robotic vacuum cleaner? First, you need to look at the problems involved. It needs to vacuum. Machines larger than the Roomba already do that, so there is some technology there to build upon, but you will have to improve upon it. It has to drive on its own, so it must have a mobility system. It has to cover the entire room without falling down stairs, missing the area under tables, or making other mistakes. It will have to be charged, because the idea of a plug trailing a vacuum cleaner around the room seems like a tangle waiting to happen. Finally, it will need to go over certain parts more than once if they're really dirty.

Looking at the problems you need to overcome is a great way to start creating your robot. The Roomba needs to "suck" up dirt like a normal vacuum cleaner, and it includes a motor that creates the vacuum suction to do that, but it also adds two spinning brushes that work in opposition, pushing the dirt toward the vacuum motor. And on the side is another brush that allows it to sweep dirt away from wall edges, table legs, and the like. Another problem is how to avoid obstacles. The original Roomba had a bumper up front that would detect a "hit" using touch sensors. Why not use more sophisticated sensors to "see" the room like infrared or ultrasonic? The answer is because they have trouble distinguishing between the skirt around the bottom of your couch and the wall. You want your vacuum to avoid a wall, while you want it to clean under your couch, if possible.

A mobility system also had to be worked out for the Roomba. It needs wheels that can drive over most household surfaces: wood, linoleum, carpet, rugs; it needs to be able to drive forward, backward, and make turns; it also needs to be low to the ground for sucking up dirt, so the wheels can't be too large. Once mobility is figured out, sensors need to be added so that the Roomba doesn't fall down stairs. The Roomba has an infrared sensor, which it calls a cliff sensor, on its bottom half that lets it know when it is approaching a drop-off so that it can stop and go the other way.

Each time a new generation of Roomba is released, it sports new features. Newer models find their way back to the charging station when their battery is low and will leave when it's fully charged. They also now feature sensors that let it know when it's going over a dirty spot that may need more than one pass. And you can set beacons at the edge of rooms to create an infrared barrier that will signal the Roomba to stop at the room's edge. The most recent model now comes with Wi-Fi and is fully programmable with an app on your smartphone.

THE PARTS OF A ROOMBA

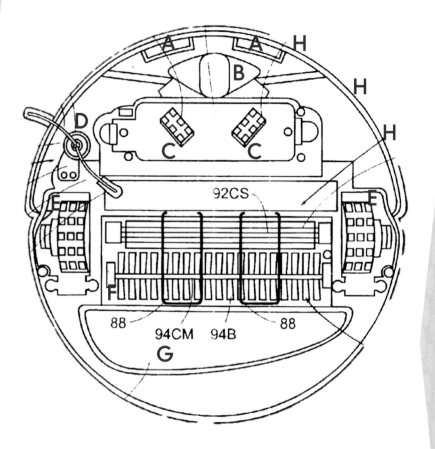

A. Infrared "cliff" sensors for sensing drop-offs.

B. Nose wheel.

C. Battery charging points.

D. Side brush for dirt near walls.

E. Motor-driven wheels.

F. Opposite rolling brushes.

G. Dirt bin.

H. The entire front end is one large bumper with sensors to detect collisions.

Path to Success

What interests me the most about the Roomba and what I think is the best takeaway for students is not the newest features but how it came up with its original algorithm for covering a room, especially one that has chairs, TV stands, tables, and odd shapes. Most of us would expect the Roomba to go back and forth, sort of the way most people vacuum or mow the lawn. But the Roomba follows an entirely different path altogether.

At first glance the time-lapse photo on page 88 seems totally random. But listen to the words of Nancy Dussault Smith, vice-president of marketing communications for iRobot, in an interview with BotJunkie:

"Our robot computes its algorithm sixty-seven times every second, constantly stitching together information about its environment and recomputing its path. When it starts you'll notice a spiral pattern, it'll spiral out over a larger and larger area until it hits an object. When it finds an object, it will follow along the edge of that object for a period of time, and then it will start crisscrossing, trying to figure out the largest distance it can go without hitting another object, and that's helping it figure out how large the space is, but if it goes for too long a period of time without hitting a wall, it's going to start spiraling again, because it figures it's in a wide open space, and it's constantly calculating and figuring that out. It's similar with the dirt sensors underneath; when one of those sensors gets tripped it changes its behaviors to cover that area. It will then go off in search of another dirty area in a straight path. The way

This time-lapse photo of the Roomba shows what looks like a completely random pattern but is actually a complex algorithm for efficient cleaning.

that these different patterns pile on to each other as they go, we know that this is the most effective way to cover a room. The patterns that we chose and how the algorithm was originally developed was based off of behavior-based algorithms born out of MIT studying animals and how they go about searching areas for food. When you look at how ants and bees go out and they search areas, these kinds of coverage and figuring all of that out comes from that research. It's not exact, obviously, I'm not saying we're honeybees, but it's that understanding of how to search out an area in nature that is the basis behind how our adaptive technology is developed."

I am absolutely stunned by the way the algorithm (set of instructions) was written for this robot to cover the area most effectively. By mimicking the behavior of animals like bees, it was able to create an algorithm that makes the Roomba drive in what looks like a wildly random pattern but is actually quite efficient. While this may not be practical for every challenge your robot is up against, it is a great model for the type of thinking that can be used in solving problems in almost any engineering setting, including, of course, robotics.

Conclusion

In summary, let's see how the Roomba itself compares to the approach we've taken in this book, specifically the last chapter, when it comes to creating robots. We have a structural system that meets our needs. It houses all of our components in a protective shell and is small enough not to be inconvenient. It has a mobility system that does what it is designed for: move over surfaces, change directions, turn around, and not get tangled in carpeting. It uses two motors to turn its wheels and has a third wheel for stability. It has actuators (components that convert electrical energy into motion) in its rollers and brushes. It uses sensors to recognize when it's bumping into things, when it's about to fall down stairs, where its charging station is, and when it has gone over an extra-dirty patch. It has a detachable battery and circuit board that comprise its control system, and though I'm not 100 percent sure, I would guess that the location of these was not the primary concern but was determined around the motors, wheels, actuators, and sensors.

A simple mat like this with different colored lines can help students practice beginning programming concepts.

5 Programming the Robot

```
10 Print "Hello"
20 GoTo 10
```

That was the first program I ever wrote on my old Atari 800 personal computer way back in the early 1980s, when I was still in elementary school. While I didn't realize it then, I had actually used some of the same programming features we are going to cover in this book. The command lines are numbered and sequential, and I incorporated a forever loop to cause the word "Hello" to print itself infinitely on my screen, or at least until I got tired and made it stop.

It can be argued that there is no one part of building and designing a robot that is more important than any other. Structure, mobility, sensors, actuators, brain—they're all needed to make the robot move and do things. But without programming, you just have a hunk of metal and plastic. A really cool looking hunk of metal and plastic, but nonetheless one that doesn't do much of anything.

All programming starts from basic, easy-to-follow steps like the ones above, and then becomes increasingly complex, involving more actions, steps, decisions, sensor readings, and movements. It's important to understand that complex is not the same as complicated. "Complex" means there's a lot going on in your program, while "complicated" means you've written your program in a really confusing manner with more steps than are needed and with inefficient commands.

We will strive to write our programs so they are efficient, clear, and easy to follow, but also able to make our robot do complex and cool things. One way to start doing this is with the use of algorithms.

An algorithm is a set of instructions for accomplishing a task. A good algorithm not only states the steps needed to complete a task clearly, it also helps us understand how to "think like a robot." In the last chapter, we talked about how robots have no sense of self-preservation and will follow any command given to them, to a fault. The command doesn't have to make sense. The robot doesn't have sense in any manner akin to a human; it will just do what it's told. This can become problematic, to say the least. Let's take a look at a common algorithm and use it to illuminate this idea of thinking like a robot while we're programming.

Algorithms

Think of the steps it takes to make a peanut butter and jelly sandwich. Don't look ahead, just come up with your own before going any further.

Did you come up with something like this?

1. Take out bread, peanut butter, and jelly.

2. Pick up knife.

3. Put knife in peanut butter.

4. Spread peanut butter on a slice of bread.

5. Put knife in jelly.

6. Spread jelly on another slice of bread.

7. Put two pieces of bread together.

8. Eat.

Seems simple enough, right? Well, we left some stuff out. Where did we get that bread? What about the jelly and peanut butter? Did you open the lids of the jars? What does it mean to "put knife in?" Did we have enough on the knife before we started spreading? When did we take the bread out of the bag? What does it mean to "spread?" And which sides of the bread and in what manner are we "putting them together?"

All of these questions are things that you or I assume from experience. They don't need to be explicitly stated because we have learned them over the years. Knowing what a peanut butter and jelly sandwich is helps us understand that when you are told to put the bread together, you want to place the jelly and peanut butter sides facing each other on the inside of the sandwich. You can't make this assumption, or any others, with a robot. You have to tell it exactly what to do in each situation, including keeping itself from harm.

You or I would probably not grab a knife by the blade because we don't want to hurt ourselves. Nobody needs to tell us this. We just know it. That's because we have a sense of self-preservation. Robots don't, and they will harm themselves if we give them directions that assume they won't hurt themselves.

Basic Movements

There is a three-step process we are going to use in this chapter to write all of our programs. The first is to write the algorithm for the problem. The second is to break that algorithm down into **pseudo-code**. Pseudo-code is a list of individual steps that the robot has to perform. It takes the language of an algorithm and breaks it down into individual actions. And finally, the code is the specific commands in whatever programming language you are using. I like to think of pseudo-code as English and code as being the translation of English into a robot language.

Let's Move

Say I want my robot to drive forward for three seconds. The algorithm for this is simple enough that I have already stated it. Robot drives forward really fast for three seconds. The next step would be to write the pseudo-code for that algorithm:

Left and right motors turn on at full power
Wait three seconds
Stop

The pseudo-code lets us see if we have the moves laid out correctly before we attempt to translate into code. For this chapter, I am going to use a programming language called RobotC. RobotC is not the only educational robot language out there, and I won't even get into a discussion about what the best language is, as that is quite subjective. I'm using RobotC because it can be used for both LEGO NXT and EV3, VEX EDR and IQ, and Arduino. It also has a graphical version that many people find helpful. All of the programs in this chapter will be written with RobotC for LEGO Mindstorms EV3 using the motor and sensor setup shown on pages 98–99.

Below is both the pseudo-code and RobotC code for our three-second challenge.

Pseudo-code	RobotC code
Left and right motors turn on at full power	setMultipleMotors (100, leftWheel, rightWheel)
Wait three seconds	wait (3, seconds)
Stop	stopAllMotors ()

Let's take a closer look at these commands and the way they're written. You'll notice the command is written first using a lowercase/uppercase nomenclature, which we will discuss later. Inside parentheses are the modifiers. For our *setMultipleMotors* command, the first modifier is speed (not in miles per hour but in percentage of available power) and the second two refer to which motors to turn on at full power. The *wait* command is followed by "3" and then "seconds," denoting, obviously, how long and in what unit the robot should wait before doing the next command. Finally, *stopAllMotors* has nothing inside the parentheses as you are stopping *all* motors. But you still have to have the open and close parentheses after the command because each programming language has its own syntax rules that must be followed.

These rules can be frustrating to follow at first. They often return errors for the smallest things (a misplaced comma, for example) and can sometimes turn students off. My advice is to start small and simple, write commands over and over, and soon you'll get the hang of it. Practice does indeed make perfect.

The other rule for RobotC is that each program is contained inside braces, which look like this { at the start and this } at the end. This can be confusing because there are also brackets [ ] and parentheses ( ). Learning when to use these takes a bit of getting used to. On the right you can see how the entire program to move our robot forward at full power for three seconds looks.

There are several things to notice and pay attention to here. The first is the generation of all the *#pragma* commands at the top for the motors and sensors, which happens automatically. I am not going to include these in the rest of the programs in this chapter as we are going to use the same setup and there's no need to take up space printing the same thing over and over. The second thing to notice here is the *task main ()* at the beginning. This is also always generated automatically at the beginning of your program. And after that we have an open brace on its own line, and at the end we have a close brace on its own line. The entire program is written in between these

```
#pragma config (Sensor, S1, touchSensor, sensorEV3_Touch)
#pragma config (Sensor, S2, ultrasonicSensor,
        sensorEV3_Ultrasonic)
#pragma config (Sensor, S3, colorSensor, sensorEV3_Color)
#pragma config (Sensor, S4, soundSensor, sensorSoundDBA)
#pragma config (Motor, motorA, armMotor, tmotorEV3_Large,
        PIDControl, encoder)
#pragma config (Motor, motorB, leftWheel, tmotorEV3_Large,
        PIDControl, driveLeft, encoder)
#pragma config (Motor, motorC, rightWheel,
        tmotorEV3_Large, PIDControl, driveRight, encoder)
//*!! Code automatically generated by 'ROBOTC'
        configuration wizard !!*//

task main ()
{
setMultipleMotors (100, leftWheel, rightWheel) ;
wait (3, seconds) ;
stopAllMotors () ;
}
```

two braces. As we will see later, more braces will be used to denote loops, *if* statements, and *while* statements. Also notice that each line is ended by a semicolon. Without that semicolon, RobotC will assume your command continues on the next line as if there's no space between them.

We are not going to pay too close attention to the syntax used here. Each programming language (Java, C+, Python, Basic, etc.) has its own syntax. And for each new programming language you learn, there will be a curve as

SETTING UP YOUR MOTORS AND SENSORS

Most programming languages require you to state ahead of time which ports the motors and sensors on your robot are connected to. They will also give you the option of naming the ports for easy recognition later. There is a temptation to get overly complicated and/or cutesy with port names, and this can cause problems later; use names that are easy to remember and make sense. Finally, the protocol for naming motors and sensors is to use two words without a space, capitalizing the first letter of the second word. For example *sweepMotor* would be the correct way to name the motor attached to your robot that is being used to sweep something. The screenshots below and on the next page are from the Motor and Sensor setup window in RobotC.

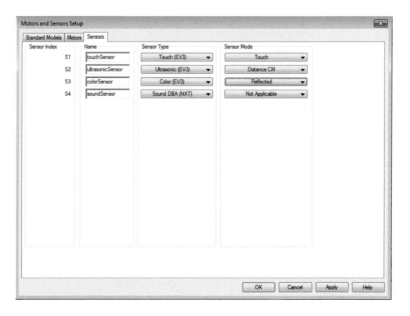

The image above shows the correct way for naming sensors plugged into specific ports.

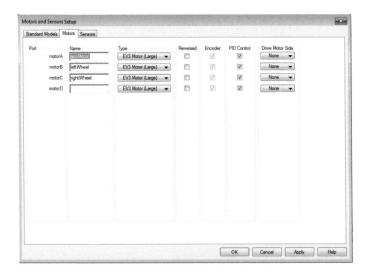

Proper naming of motors can remove any confusion as to which motor will respond to commands in your program.

```
#pragma config (Sensor, S1, touchSensor, sensorEV3_Touch)
#pragma config (Sensor, S2, ultrasonicSensor,
        sensorEV3_Ultrasonic)
#pragma config (Sensor, S3, colorSensor, sensorEV3_Color)
#pragma config (Sensor, S4, soundSensor, sensorSoundDBA)
#pragma config (Motor, motorA, armMotor, tmotorEV3_Large,
        PIDControl, encoder)
#pragma config (Motor, motorB, leftWheel, tmotorEV3_Large,
        PIDControl, driveLeft, encoder)
#pragma config (Motor, motorC, rightWheel,
        tmotorEV3_Large, PIDControl, driveRight, encoder)
//*!! Code automatically generated by 'ROBOTC'
        configuration wizard !!*//
```

Once you've set up your motors and sensors, the program will populate a bunch of standard code lines, as in the example above. Once these appear at the top of your program, you don't have to worry about them.

you adjust to the new rules. For now, keep this in mind: each language has to have a way of distinguishing one command from another (semicolons are used here), each program has a way of indicating when a program starts and finishes (the use of braces), and each program will have a way of denoting structures, subroutines, and the like (again the use of braces). It may be frustrating, but we're not going to pay close attention to the syntax as it changes often. What does not change are the basic concepts which underlie programming. And those are what we are going to focus on going forward.

One of the easiest ways to learn syntax is to look at sample programs that have already been written in that language. By clicking File>Open Sample Programs in RobotC, you are treated to a folder that looks like this:

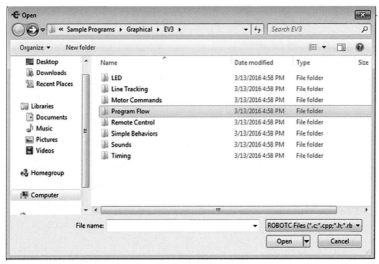

By looking in folders for already written programs, you can begin to learn their structure.

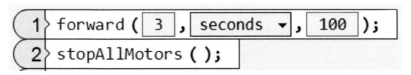

```
1  forward ( 3 , seconds ▾ , 100 );
2  stopAllMotors ( );
```

There are multiple ways to write the same program.

And within each of those subfolders are numerous programs. You can use them to learn syntax and see how different commands are used. I admit to peeking at a few programs to refresh my memory while writing this chapter.

One of the reasons I enjoy teaching robotics is there is always more than one solution to a given problem. For example, I used a *setMultipleMotors* command in the last program. I could have as easily used a different command to accomplish the same thing. In the case above, RobotC has a few commands that make a few basic assumptions about what you want to do. For example the *forward* command is often used when you want to drive forward, as we did. It assumes you have two motors attached to two drive wheels on either side of your robot.

You will also notice that this program has the duration (three seconds) built into it so there is no need to follow the command where you are moving the motors with a command to wait for three seconds. So which way is better to use? For the most part, the simplest command is usually the best. Objectively it uses less memory—though in this case it's a negligible difference—and that can be important when you have a very long program. It's also one fewer command, and that means one less place where things can go wrong. On the other hand, there are some programmers who like to control each action individually. They don't like to give up control to an uber command that takes care of all the little pieces.

There's some logic to this as it helps to know what's going on with your robot right down to the last detail, especially if you want it to be successful. Knowing that you have to turn two motors on for a specified duration in order to make your robot move gives you a greater feeling of control than just telling it to go forward. For my part, I will be happy if you can get your robot to do what you want it to do without worrying about which programming style is the best.

Let's add a level of complexity to our programming by requiring our robot to drive in a 2-foot (0.6 m) square, stopping and starting as close to the same spot as possible. There are several things I need to figure out in order to program this challenge. The first is going to be how far (for what duration) the robot needs to drive in order to go 2 feet? Then I need to know what type of turn I need to make and again for what duration. Once I have this all figured out, I need to work on writing a program that repeats itself four times. Let's take a look at the algorithm and pseudo-code for this program before we tackle the individual parts.

Algorithm
Drive forward for 2 feet.
Turn 90 degrees.
Repeat four times.

Pseudo-code

Reset the **motor encoder** on right motor.

Turn on both drive motors at half power.

Wait until the motor encoder reads 1,270.8 degrees.

Stop motors.

Wait half a second.

Reset the motor encoder on right motor.

Turn the right motor on at half power.

Wait for the motor encoder to read 332.64 degrees.

Stop the motor.

Wait half a second.

Repeat 4 times.

There's a lot there in eleven pseudo-code commands. Let's break it down one step at a time. The first command is to reset the motor encoder on the right motor. This is because I am going to use the encoder to count rotations, which I will use to determine when my robot has gone forward 2 feet. How did I calculate this? First of all, I am using the regular EV3 tires, which measure 5.5 centimeters in diameter. So just as I did with a different-sized wheel in chapter 4, I am going to use diameter, pi, circumference, and the known distance to determine how long I need to go forward for. If my diameter is 5.5 centimeters, I multiply that by pi (3.14) to determine the tire circumference, which in this case is 17.27 centimeters. Two feet converts to 60.96 centimeters, which is my known distance. If I divide my known distance (60.96 cm) by the distance my robot travels in one rotation (17.27 cm), the answer is 3.53. Finally I have to multiply this by 360 because the *getMotorEncoder* command I am going to use later only counts degrees, not rotations. This is the duration I need to turn my motors on in order to drive forward for 2 feet. The next command is to stop and then wait half a second. I could just go directly into the turn command, but I wished to stop and wait first. I do this for a few reasons. First, I always like to have pauses in my program to see what my robot is doing. If my robot continuously goes from one movement to another, it is often very difficult to tell where a mistake has been made. By pausing between movements, I am able to see what my robot is doing, and it is easier to catch mistakes. I also like to pause when I am going from one movement to a radically different one. Sometimes momentum from one action can affect the next one. By stopping and waiting before I turn, I allow my robot to rest so there is no carry-over in momentum from the straight to the turn.

At this point I will reset my motor encoder again as it has just been read for the forward movement. I could use the left encoder for my forward movements and my right encoder for the turns, but I prefer to stick with one and reset it each time I am going to count again. The next step was to try to figure out what type of turn to make. There are basically two options here: I can make a point turn or a swing turn. A point turn is when my robot travels around a center point. A point turn will work best when the center of my robot is located between my two drive wheels. If my drive wheels are too far forward or back from the center point of my robot, a point turn won't work. To execute a point turn, one wheel will turn backward and the opposite wheel will turn forward, both at the same speed. The robot will appear to turn around a center point of the robot. I choose not to use a point turn for two reasons. The first is there seems to be more slippage in real life when attempting this type of turn with two rubber tires on a surface like a competition mat or a classroom floor. There just is. The second reason is it's harder to calculate how much duration to program in order to make a particular degree turn. It is for this reason that I prefer a swing turn.

A swing turn, sometimes called a pivot turn, is when the outside wheel swings around the stationary inside wheel. So if our right motor turns, we will swing around our left wheel, making a left turn. This turn has the advantage of using some really cool math to determine how much we need to program our wheel to turn in order to make a 90-degree turn. Here's how to do it:

1. First we need to measure the wheelbase; this is the distance between the center of our left wheel and the center of our right wheel. In the robot I am using for this program, the wheelbase is 4 inches.

2. Picture in your mind (use the diagram on page 106 to help) that the stationary (left) wheel is the center of a circle whose radius is 4 inches. This means that the diameter is 8 inches. I am going to convert this to centimeters since those are the units I have already used to calculate my wheel circumference. Eight inches converts to 20.32 centimeters.

3. If the diameter of my circle is 20.32 centimeters, then I can multiply that by pi to figure out its circumference: 20.32 cm x 3.14 cm = 63.8 cm.

4. Now that I know the circle with my tire at the center has a circumference of 63.8 cm, I know how far my outer wheel would have to travel to make it around that entire circle. But I am only going one-quarter of the way around. My robot is making a 90-degree turn, remember? So I will divide 63.8 by 4, which gives me 15.95 centimeters. So my outer wheel has to drive for 15.95 cm. I already know how far my robot travels in one rotation—17.27 centimeters—so I once again divide the distance I have to travel by my wheel circumference. When 15.95 is divided by 17.27, you get 0.924. And again, I will have to multiply that number by 360 to convert from rotations to degrees. So that is the duration I would have to program my robot's motors to turn for.

4-inch radius = 8-inch diameter.
8 inches converts to 20.32 cm
20.32 cm x 3.14 (pi) = 63.8 cm
63.8 / 4 = 15.95 cm for the
   90-degree turn
15.95 / 17.27 = 0.924 rotations
0.924 x 360 = 332.64 (convert
   rotations to degrees)

The wheelbase and the wheel's circumference are critical factors.

All that math for one line of code! After our motor encoder reads the duration of 332.64, we again stop the motors and wait for half a second. And finally we will repeat the program four times because there are four sides to a square.

Here's what that program would look like:

```
task main ()
{
    repeat (4) {
        resetMotorEncoder () ;
        setMotor (leftWheel, 50) ;
        setMotor (rightWheel, 50) ;
        waitUntil (getMotorEncoder (rightWheel) == 1,270.8) ;
        stopAllMotors () ;
        wait (.5, seconds) ;
        resetMotorEncoder (rightWheel) ;
        setMotor (rightWheel, 50) ;
        waitUntil (getMotorEncoder (rightWheel) == 332.64) ;
        stopMotor (rightWheel) ;
        wait (.5, seconds) ;
    }
}
```

I left the motor configuration out of the program because that will always be the same for this chapter. We start with the same *task main ()* command and an open brace. Pay attention to the brace. Its match (close brace) is down in the last line of the program. You can see that neither of the braces in these lines is indented. This is an easy indication that they are a pair. Now move forward to the end of the line with the *repeat (4)* command. This is the beginning of our loop. And the parts of the program (in this case the entire program) that will repeat are after this brace and before the second-to-last brace.

In between you'll see a list of commands that pretty much matches our pseudo-code line for line. All of the commands are written in blue, and all of the variables are written in reds. As a programmer, you don't have to worry about this; RobotC does it automatically in order to help you distinguish between one and the other. The double equal sign is used to denote that you are waiting for a statement to be true, not expressing a true equality. For example: (getMotorEncoder (rightMotor) == 1,270.8).

A semicolon follows each command, as was the case in the last program, except for the repeat command. Repeat is not a command to the robot to do anything, but it is what is called a program structure. This structure is followed by the brace that indicates everything between it and the matched close brace on the second-to-last line is to be repeated four times.

Using Sensors

You may not have realized it, but we have already used sensors in this chapter. We used the motor encoders to drive in a square in the last section. The motor encoder is not often thought of as a sensor as it is not an additional piece of hardware that you have to plug in to your robot, but is part of the motor itself. It is a sensor nevertheless as it gives us information about its environment.

Let's start with the touch sensor and a simple program that uses the *waitUntil* command. Let's say you want to use a touch sensor to start and stop your robot. You could do this simply enough by including *wait* commands in a loop. The pseudo-code would read like this:

Wait for the touch sensor to be pushed.

Start the robot.

Wait for the touch sensor to be pushed.

Stop the robot.

Loop.

Here's how we would write that program:

```
task main ()
{
    repeat (forever)  {
        waitUntil (getTouchValue (touchSensor) == true) ;
        // when the touch sensor is pushed
        setMultipleMotors (50, leftWheel, rightWheel) ;
        // turn the motors on
        waitUntil (getTouchValue (touchSensor) == true) ;
        // when the touch sensor is pushed again
        stopMultipleMotors (leftWheel, rightWheel) ;
        // turn the motors off
    }
}
```

You should see some familiar commands here. Two things that may be new are the use of *true* and the use of comments. The true condition for the touch sensors refer to them being in the on position. Remember, a touch sensor has only two states, on and off. If it is on (if it is pushed in), then its condition is true. And if it is off (not pushed in), then its condition is false. The other new concept in this program is that of commenting.

Comments are something that most programmers use. They can remind a programmer of what a particular command is supposed to do or of what a value or number is supposed to represent. They can also supply information to other people that may be looking at your code and trying to figure out what it is supposed to mean. In most programming environments, RobotC included, you use two slashes (//) to denote that what is following is a comment and not part of the program. In RobotC, those comments are turned to green for easy viewing.

Another way to use a sensor is to use an *if* statement. An *if* statement is similar to *waitUntil* in that they are both assuming or anticipating information from a sensor. But while the *waitUntil* statement assumes that specific information will be coming, the *if* statement is just preparing for the possibility.

In the following program, the loop will check to see if an item is closer than 4 inches (10 cm). If it is, then the robot will back away for two rotations, then go on to the next command, which in this case is to repeat the loop. If there isn't an object, then the robot will skip out of the *if* statement and go on to the next command, which is also the loop. This way the program will continuously check for close objects and back up if they appear.

```
task main ()
{
    repeat (forever) {
        if (getUSDistance (distanceSensor) < 10) {
            backward (2, rotations, 50) ;
        }
        stopAllMotors () ;
    }
}
```

An *if* statement has only one condition, and if you don't meet that condition, you exit out of the statement to the rest of the program. There is another option that allows you to choose one course of action if a statement is met and a different course of action if that statement is not met. This is called an *if else* statement. One of the most common uses of *if else* statements is in line following.

Line following is a popular beginning programming challenge. You use the color sensor to read the difference in reflection between the surface and a line on it. This setup can be accomplished with a white table and a black line made using a piece of electrical tape. The color sensor can be used to detect the reflection of light off of different surfaces. It will read higher numbers off of bright surfaces that reflect more light and lower numbers off of darker surfaces. The color sensor reads scaled values from 1 to 100. Every surface will reflect different numbers, but if you are using white and black, you will usually receive a number higher than 50 for white and lower than 50 for black. Therefore we will use 50 as what is called a threshold for our program.

A threshold is a number which, when passed, will trigger a certain event. We use 50 as our threshold because it is a median number. It is not close to the high number that we would read on the white surface, nor the low number from the black tape. And we don't want it to be close to those numbers. Readings fluctuate and can change with a bit of bright light or a shadow cast from a human hand.

In this program, our robot will continue to follow a line until our ultrasonic sensor sees something that is closer than

THRESHOLD TIP

It's important that we don't rely on readings to stay absolute but rather choose a threshold that is close neither to our high nor to our low number.

10 centimeters (4 inches), then it will stop. In order to run this program, we need to line up our robot so that the color sensor starts just to the left of the line. Here's what the pseudo-code looks like:

> If you see dark
>> Turn off the left motor
>> Turn on the right motor
>
> If you see light
>> Turn off the right motor
>> Turn on the left motor
>
> Continue doing this until there is an object less than
>> 10 centimeters (4 inches) away.

As our programs get more and more complex, it is harder to write pseudo-code that accurately reflects what the program does. Our program won't sequentially look for light then dark, it will just read the color sensor and then make a decision based on the result. This program appears at the top of the next page.

You can also use *if else* statements to have your robot carry out different actions based on several different conditions rather than just one or two. We'll use the color sensor again for this example, but we'll use it in its color mode. Imagine you have built a robot that sorts colored pieces of candy. One motor runs

```
task main ()
{
    repeatUntil (getUSDistance (distanceSensor) < 10) {
        if (getColorReflected (colorSensor) < 50) {
                stopMotor (leftWheel) ;
                setMotor (rightWheel, 50) ;
        }       else  {
                stopMotor (rightWheel) ;
                setMotor (leftWheel, 50) ;
        }
    }
    stopAllMotors () ;
}
```

a conveyor belt along which the candy travels. As the candy pieces pass the color sensor, it uses its color mode to read the color of each piece and then opens one of a series of gates for the candy to pass through.

The motor and sensor setup for this program would have to be written to reflect that there is a color sensor and that three different motors are operating three different gates. You can see the code for this example on the next page.

While this program may look complex, it follows some patterns that should be easily discernible, as you have made it this far in the book. I have added two comments to make the first part of the program clear, but after that it just repeats itself. The conveyor belt starts right away and never stops. The color sensor is looking for different colors. The first condition I put in was black as that is the color of the conveyor belt and the color that will probably be seen most often. If black is seen, then the robot should do nothing other than continue on with the conveyor belt.

```
task main ()
{
    repeat (forever)  {
        setMotor (conveyorMotor, 50) ;
        if (getColorName (colorSensor) == colorBlack) {
            // Do nothing if it is black. This is the color of the
conveyor belt.
        } else {
        if (getColorName (colorSensor) == colorBlue) {
            moveMotor (gate1Motor, .25, rotations, 25) ;
            wait (3, seconds) ;
            moveMotor (gate1Motor, -.25, rotations, 25) ;
            // If it sees blue, then open the first gate for 3
seconds, then close it.
        } else {
        if (getColorName (colorSensor) == colorGreen) {
            moveMotor (gate2Motor, .25, rotations, 25) ;
            wait (3, seconds) ;
            moveMotor (gate2Motor, -.25, rotations, 25) ;
        } else {
        if (getColorName (colorSensor) == colorYellow) {
            moveMotor (gate3Motor, .25, rotations, 25) ;
            wait (3, seconds) ;
            moveMotor (gate3Motor, -.25, rotations, 25) ;
        } else {
        }
        }
        }
        }
    }
}
```

If the color is blue, then one gate will open slightly for three
seconds. If it is not blue then the color sensor will check to see if
it's green and open up a different gate, and if it's yellow a third gate

will open and close. You could continue this pattern for as many different colors (EV3 will read seven different ones) as you have.

You may also notice that I used a *moveMotor* command in some places as opposed to a *setMotor* command. The difference here is that with *setMotor* you are just turning your motors on and then will have to turn them off later after a duration which you must specify, with a *wait for time* command, for example. A *moveMotor* command, on the other hand, allows you to specify the type of duration, the length of duration, and the power. This way I was able to open and close each motor for a quarter of a rotation at a low power (25) all in one command.

Conclusion

This chapter has covered a few of the basic and most common programming techniques. It would be impossible to cover them all in one book, but if you follow the strategies I have laid out, you should do fine. Always begin with an algorithm that explains what it is you want your robot to do to meet a certain challenge. Then break that down into individual steps your robot can take by creating pseudo-code. And finally, translate the pseudo-code into whatever programming language you are using. If you get stuck, check the help section of your program; it usually contains a very good explanation of what the commands mean. Some programs, like RobotC, contain sample code for most situations that you can adapt to whatever program you're writing. And finally, check online. There are forums dedicated to all sorts of programming languages, and it's a good solid bet you will be able to find the answers you're looking for.

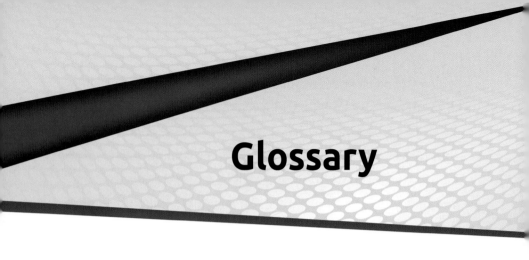

Glossary

accelerometer A sensor that can sense tilt in three directions, along the x, y, and z axes.

actuators Any mechanism that turns energy (usually electric, hydraulic, or pneumatic) into motion.

algorithm A set of instructions for accomplishing a task.

ambient light The amount of light in a given area.

analog sensor A sensor that has an infinite range of values, like a potentiometer that increases infinitely as it is turned.

anthropomorphic robot A robot that has features similar to a human being.

auto-identification The ability of some robots to detect which sensors and motors are plugged into which ports without being told by the programmer.

axle A long shaft used for connecting motors, wheels, and other structural pieces.

beam A structural piece usually with holes used for building the foundation of most robots.

bearings Parts used in VEX to provide a round opening for the square shafts.

bending A force that acts upon a point on a fixed structural piece. Bending involves compression on top and tension on the bottom.

bevel gear A round gear that has teeth angled so that the gears can be connected at angles other than 180.

bushings Pieces used to hold wheels onto axles and space them from the body so as to minimize rubbing.

color sensor A sensor that senses different colors and in some cases reflected light.

compression Opposite forces pushing toward one point.

continuous rotation servos A type of servo motor that rotates in either direction continuously rather than to a fixed point.

controller The part in a robot that connects and controls power, sensors, and motors.

control system The battery or other power source and the controller on a robot.

cross bracing A method of building that uses pieces to support a structure by crossing at an angle.

DC motor A motor that runs on direct current by adjusting current speed, while exact positioning is hard to maintain.

degrees of freedom The number of independent ways a rigid body can move.

digital sensor A sensor whose values are output in discreet increments.

drone An unmanned aircraft or ship, controlled either remotely or via onboard guidance computers.

educational robot A robot designed for use in educational settings, usually small, inexpensive, easily programmable, and capable of being modified into different configurations.

Faraday cage A metal cage that blocks certain signals like radio waves or Wi-Fi.

gear A part that is toothed and used to connect with others to transmit or change motion, directions, speed, or power.

graphical programming environment A programming environment for robots that contains graphical blocks or icons that are linked to create a program.

gyro sensor A sensor that measures angular momentum.

hydraulic A machine or mechanism using liquid power; hydraulics are strong because it is hard to compress liquids.

inertia The tendency of a body to resist a change in its velocity. If it is at rest, it will stay that way until acted upon; if it is moving, it will continue to move until acted upon.

lead screw A mechanism often used in a linear actuator consisting of a fixed, threaded rod and a nut; the nut and any parts attached to it move horizontally as the rod is turned.

linear actuator An actuator that turns the energy into linear motion.

mobility system The parts of the robot involved in motion, such as motors, wheels, gears, axles, shafts, etc.

motor encoder A sensor placed inside a motor that can measure the degrees of rotation.

omni-wheel A wheel that has intermittent rollers that move perpendicularly to the main direction of rotation of the wheel.

piston The moving piece in hydraulic and pneumatic pumps that creates the internal pressure.

pneumatic A machine or mechanism using compressed gas power; pneumatics can provide very accurate motion.

port The connection point on controllers for motors and sensors.

pseudo-code A listing of individual steps a robot must take to complete a task.

rack and pinion A mechanism consisting of a spur gear (pinion) and a long, vertical-toothed gear (rack) wherein the pinion turns, causing the rack to move in a linear motion.

reflected light The amount of light that reflects off of a given surface.

robot A programmable machine built to carry out a task or series of tasks automatically.

Roomba A brand of robotic vacuums produced by the company iRobot.

scissor lift A mechanism with diagonally crossed beams connected in their centers and raised by a linear actuator.

servo motor A motor that turns to a specific location; most servo motors turn between 0 and 90 or 180 degrees.

shaft A long vertical piece, square in its profile, used to connect motors and wheels.

shear A force that pushes or pulls on adjacent, but not directly opposite, parts of a structure or piece.

sound sensor A sensor that detects sound, usually measuring it in decibels.

spur gear Any type of round gear with teeth.

structural foundation The part of the robot that holds it together and gives it strength, shape, and form.

syntax The correct use of punctuation and capitalization in text-based programming.

tension A force that pulls in opposite directions.

text-based Describing any programming language that uses words and punctuation.

torque Power in a circular motion.

torsion A twisting force on an object.

touch sensor A sensor that senses a push or release.

universal joint A mechanism that allows the input and output forces to be between 90 and 270 degrees.

Further Information

Competition Websites

FIRST Robotic Competition

www.firstinspires.org

This site is the clearinghouse for all FIRST competitions from Jr. FLL to FRC. You can find rules, registration, and area event information here.

High Tech Kids

www.hightechkids.org

This site, run by volunteers in the state of Minnesota, provides free resources and training for teams competing in FLL and other competitions. It is the first site I went to over a decade ago when I started coaching FIRST LEGO League.

International Robot Olympiad

www.iroc.org

One of the most popular robotics competitions, IROC is for children under the age of eight to college undergraduates.

National Robotics Challenge

www.thenrc.org

This event is not connected to an organization, so there is no kit to buy. Students are challenged to find materials to best achieve their solutions.

Robotics Education and Competition Foundation

www.roboticseducation.org

The Robotics Education Foundation provides two separate competitions for VEX IQ and VEX EDR robots.

Instructional Websites

Carnegie Mellon Robotics Academy

education.rec.ri.cmu.edu

The Carnegie Mellon Robotics Academy home page provides links to resources for students and teachers for both VEX and LEGO formats.

Damien Kee's Technology in Education Page

www.damienkee.com

Damien Kee has been a leader in educational robotics for over a decade now. He has written several books on robotics and his design for Riley Rover is used in hundreds of classrooms (including mine) around the world. I highly suggest you join his robotics email group (sign up from his site).

Ian Chow-Miller's YouTube Page

www.youtube.com/ianchowmiller

There are hundreds of videos on Ian Chow-Miller's YouTube page, many of which help illuminate a lot of the topics covered in this book.

LEGO Education Community

community.education.lego.com

LEGO Education has provided this community forum to help its users question, explore, share, and communicate their ideas with each other and with LEGO Education employees.

LEGO Engineering

www.legoengineering.com

Hosted by Tufts University Center for Engineering Education and Outreach (CEEO), this site contains hundreds of articles pertaining to the world of robotics education. The author of this book is a contributor.

LEGO MINDSTORMS Blog

www.thenxtstep.com

This blog didn't change its name when LEGO created the EV3 line, but it is very current with information related to the EV3 as well as other issues in robotics.

RobotShop Blog

www.robotshop.com/blog/en

Blog posts cover an array of robotics issues, from building a simple robot to programming in different languages.

STEM Education with a Robotics Implementation

stemrobotics.cs.pdx.edu/node/291

This site provides curriculum for robotics classes. The curriculum is free and customizable and anyone with a (free) account can add to it or remix different parts into their own.

Product Websites

Andymark

www.andymark.com

Andymark is a robotics part supplier with many good options for motors, actuators, servos, etc. Andymark is a sponsor of FIRST Robotics and supplies many of the items in the kit of parts.

LEGO Education

www.legoeducation.us

In the USA, this is the site for purchasing all LEGO Mindstorms robots and related products.

McMaster-Carr

www.mcmaster.com

McMaster-Carr is a huge supplier of all things fabrication and manufacturing. This site is good for looking up off the shelf odds and ends or even for purchasing raw materials.

Mindsensors

www.mindsensors.com

One of the companies that makes third-party sensors for EV3 robots, including a line of cameras.

RobotShop

www.robotshop.com

This online shop can provide you with parts for your robot or with some of the latest high-tech toys.

VEX Robotics

www.vexrobotics.com

This is the site to purchase all VEX Robotics materials including the EDR and IQ lines.

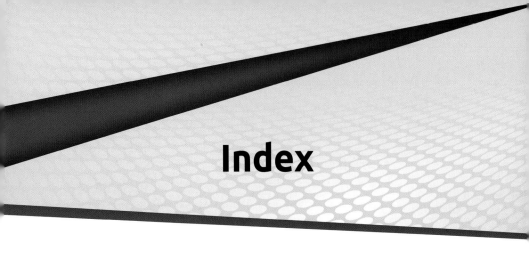

Index

About the Author

Ian Chow-Miller is a New York native who has lived in Tacoma, Washington, for the past eight years. He began his career as a social studies teacher but switched to robotics a decade ago and hasn't looked back. He has written curriculum for robotics and trained teachers around the country. He is a member of the LEGO Educator's Advisory Panel and is a constant contributor to Tufts University's LEGO Engineering website. Ian has coached FIRST LEGO League consistently since 2004, and when robotics season ends, he starts coaching soccer. He is married to an awesome wife and has two great sons who are budding engineers.